bangkok to Ben Nevis Backwards!

a journey through Dementia, from England to Scotland, India, Thailand, and back

PHIL HALL

BANGKOK TO BEN NEVIS BACKWARDS!

Copyright © 2018 by Philips Hall
Cover illustration by Jana Nenedic
Photos used for cover illustration:
Shutterstock: Bertl123/Alexandre Chambon

Philip Hall has asserted his right under the
Copyright, Designs and Patents Act 1988
to be identified as the author of this work.

All rights reserved. No part of this book may be reproduced, stored in or introduced into a retrieval system, or transmitted by any means without the prior written approval of the author of this publication.

This book is sold subject to the condition that it shall not be lent, resold, hired out, or otherwise circulated by any means in any form or binding or cover other than that in which it is published and without the same condition being imposed on the subsequent purchaser, without the publisher's prior consent.

First published in Great Britain in 2017 by
ScriptCraft Publishing
(a division of Sunpenny Limited)

Third Edition

SCRIPTCRAFT
PROFESSIONAL PUBLISHING SERVICES
SUNPENNY PUBLISHING GROUP

bangkok to BEN NEVIS BACKWARDS!

by

PHIL HALL

dedications

To my lovely wife Jum: without you none of this would have been possible. Thanks for being my own personal Ben Nevis!

To my awesome son Tom: you really rock, dude, and you simply are the best of me!

To Megan: you adorable companion who is always there for us.

To my dear Dad: you are in a better place now old soldier.

To Mum, such a strong and wise lady.

Contents

Prologue 1
Time for Change? 5
On Our Way 21
Saying goodbye... for the last time? 39
Good Morning India 47
Plan B 63
The Land of Smiles 71
The Boy, the Girl, the Fish and the Spider 77
How These People Roll 95
We Are Family 105
The People's Democratic Republic of Laos 113
Teaching 125
Entertainer or Educator? 151
Teaching in Thailand – My Opinion 157
The Man from Delta Force and other indiscretions . . 169
A Call for Help / Saying Goodbye to New Friends . . 181
Homeward Bound 189
What We've Become 207
About the Author 234

prologue

If you've ever watched the Tom Hanks film 'Terminal', well – that's kind of how myself and Jum first met. Okay, I wasn't an Eastern European businessman, and neither did Jum look much like Catherine Zeta-whatsername (Jum was far cuter IMO). However, we did meet in an airport and I suppose that is as a romantic place as any for a first encounter.

It was 1997. I was at Don Muang airport in Bangkok, just about to fly back to the UK. It being mid-December, I wasn't really looking forward to returning to a cold, wet, grey country and a small flat in North London. My Thai holiday had been a short one, but I'd enjoyed the break and now it was time to face reality again.

I was 30 years old and although I had a decent job, my life as a single man was pretty lonely to say the least. Most of my good friends had long since found their soulmates and settled down. The people I hung around with were either borderline alcoholics or work colleagues with equally dull and empty personal lives.

I looked around the airport and could see hundreds of facsimiles of myself, if a little older and sadder. Was this what my life was to become? Fast forward twenty years and I could see plenty of evidence that chilled me to the bone.

I soon snapped out of it as a couple of airport cleaning ladies hurried past me. The prettier of the two looked back at me and flashed a million-baht smile.

I would miss this place…

I'd already checked my luggage in and was strolling around the departure lounge killing some time before the inevitable call for my flight. The flight was around eleven

Bangkok to Ben Nevis Backwards!

hours; I'd be back in London just in time for Eastenders, or whatever tripe they served up as TV entertainment nowadays.

The airport benches weren't exactly welcoming but they would have to do, as I decided to chill for thirty minutes or so before that last stroll to the departure gate.

Jesus, I thought, this was like waiting to be called for the hangman, or the electric chair.

I was amazed at how down I was feeling; the holiday was a good one but way too short. Although I had been pretty much around the world in my thirty years, I'd stopped bothering with places like USA or Europe because they just didn't do it for me anymore. Asia was the place for me, and I vowed that one day, I would try and make this place my home.

'Ladies and Gentlemen, Flight number TG149 for London is now boarding, please come to Gate 45.'

There it was, my plane was boarding and it was time for me to shift.

The gate wasn't too far away and within a few minutes I was in the queue for boarding passes. 'Ticket and Passport please,' said the stunning air stewardess.

I fished around in my pocket and found the ticket, but my passport had disappeared.

'What the hell!'

I was cursing and could feel many pairs of eyes looking at me as I realised that my passport was definitely not there. Instead of wasting any more time I turned on my heel to leave the area – and bumped straight into the pretty airport cleaner, who must have been running at some pace because both of us fell to the floor from the impact.

As we stood up, she flashed that amazing smile again and thrust my passport and wallet in my hand. Before I could say thanks, my guardian angel turned on her heel and walked off.

The flight was uneventful but I kept wondering about that girl. My wallet still had the same amount of cash, and even my cards were intact. I knew that domestic cleaners in Thailand were paid less than a fiver per day, so the temptation of those crisp twenty pound notes must have been hard to resist. I would have gladly given her them all

Prologue

just to find out her name and a contact number.

After the uneventful flight was over I caught the airport tube and was back in Enfield, North London, in time to catch the closing credits to Eastenders.

I decided to call Mum and Dad to see how they had been. Just as I picked up the phone I noticed that the answerphone light was flashing away.

'Probably a cold caller,' I muttered to myself, pressing the 'play' button.

There was some background noise and then a giggle before the caller spoke. 'Meestah Hall, I am Jum and I call you from airport. I am very sorry to call you –'

More laughter. Clearly, she was not.

My heart skipped a beat as I realised it was my airport saviour!

Apparently, she had liberated one of my business cards from my wallet and had decided to get in touch, very quickly indeed. In fact, she had called before I'd even left the tarmac of Don Muang. This lady was nothing if not impulsive!

She was a breath of fresh air and exactly what my life had been missing.

She was Jum, soon to be the love of my life!

And soon, there would be a new member of our team.

July the 1st, 1998 at around 9 a.m. – a time I'd never forget. Thomas Colin Samran Hall was brought into the world exactly one month early. The place: Royal Berkshire Hospital in Reading.

I'd passed through this nondescript oversized town a few times, but never dreamt that it would be the setting for such an epic event. My son weighed in at just over eight pounds, very big for a premature baby. He was delivered Caesarean-style at the advice of the doctors because Jum isn't a large lady and it was looking as if Tom's weight was going to hit double figures.

I was over ten pounds myself when I was born, and Mum has never forgiven me for that!

He was a lovely baby and already had more hair than I did! Because he had a few complications with breathing, Tom was taken away to the incubator room (or whatever it was called) and stayed there for a few days, much to our dismay.

I'll never forget the second time I met my son. It was a bit farcical really; the nurse asked my name and pointed towards the incubator next to the door. Inside lay a small human, and he looked pretty active! We locked eyes for the very first time, and instantly I felt humbled.

'From now on, big guy, you are going to be our main priority!' I whispered to him in awe.

He looked back, and I noticed that Tom seemed a lot more Asian-looking than the last time I had seen him. But mixed-race babies often take after one side of the family more than the other, and I simply acknowledged that I had crap genes – no surprise there.

I was just coming to terms with this fact when an Asian couple approached, giving me an odd look.

'Excuse me sir, this is our child...'

'Ah, okay then, no worries,' I mumbled, and walked blushingly in no particular direction.

My eyes then noticed the name 'Thomas Hall' scribbled onto a white label on another incubator. I peered in and there he was, fast asleep – my slightly less Asian-looking son!

He was beautiful and still is to this very day; gentle natured, sensitive, yet strong – all I could have wished for in my handsome son.

Chapter 1

TIME FOR CHANGE?

They say that moving home is one of the most stressful things you can experience in life. Changing jobs is also right up there, and whilst we're on the subject, how about emigrating?

So how about all three, with a healthy dose of uncertainty thrown in for good measure? How did that rank on the stress-o-meter?

Pretty high I reckon, but that was exactly what the Hall family were about to take on, and then some!

We certainly didn't do anything by half measures, that much was true.

Although the hire car was pretty enormous, fitting three humans and a lively West Highland Terrier, plus what remained of our entire possessions, was proving to be more than a challenge – particularly at a little after 4 a.m. in the morning.

Each time I went back into the empty terraced house I paused to look at the 'Sold' sign beaming back at me next to the doorway. 'Subject to Contract' was also on the sign and these three little words seemed to be getting bigger each time. You see, selling a house in those days was indeed stressful, not least because the bloody thing wasn't truly sold until the day the equity hit your bank account.

My wife Jum was looking even worse than I was feeling, and I knew she had grave misgivings about this whole event. We had moved to the town of Wallingford a little over a decade ago, and she had fallen in love with the place almost immediately.

Bangkok to Ben Nevis Backwards!

What was not to like? With a population of around 8,000 souls, and nestled in the beautiful South Oxfordshire countryside with plenty of amenities on offer, not to mention decent schools and at least a dozen pubs, this place had it all. In fact, the campsite next to the River Thames attracted holidaymakers from all over Europe, although I personally thought that was stretching things a little bit!

As I was doing a last sweep of the empty house I was hit with a wave of nostalgia. Years of memories were seeped into this somewhat basic yet comfortable family home, and here we were simply upping sticks – *why?*

Well, things had kind of taken a turn for the worse in the last three years and the job offer from a software company in Bangalore had seemed like a godsend at the time.

I had worked in IT since the age of 19, and here I was at the age of 45 finally living the dream. I had always wanted to work in a foreign country, and now I finally had the chance. But it wasn't exactly the backdrop that I had envisaged. Life had thrust itself into the way of my plans – and that was putting it mildly.

Up until 2 years ago I had been earning decent money working as an IT contractor in the UNIX field. A salary of over £50,000 went a long way to keeping the Hall family nice and comfortable.

Life had been good.

Then one day the financial carpet was well and truly pulled from underneath our collective feet. The work arena was drying up and UK firms were looking to India and other low-paying off-shore regions to boost their profits.

These countries had skilled workforces who could do our jobs for a tenth of the price, so it was no real surprise when my employer, PepsiCo, had followed this route.

One morning at work I was introduced to a couple of nice Indian chaps who would eventually take away the lifestyle to which the Hall family had been accustomed. In a few short months they had picked up the ball and had run five or six thousand miles with it, along with my healthy pay packet.

PepsiCo were nothing if not considerate employers; however, after a few months of looking for work I was called by one of my former managers. There was a position on the

Time for Change?

IT service desk and they wanted me for the job!

I was desperate and said yes almost immediately, but when I looked at the starting salary my heart sank. Less than half of my old wages, plus the fact I was going to be doing a job that was entry level at best. My bank manager was not going to be pleased, and neither would the mortgage company.

Since living in Norman Way, Wallingford, I had not exactly been clever with my earnings, and although Jum had worked her socks off her own wages wouldn't even cover the monthly food bill. But that was no excuse for the debts that had piled up slowly but surely.

So I swallowed what was left of my pride and started back at the soft drinks giant, albeit in a less skilled role.

I was at least twenty years older than the rest of the team – even my manager was ten years younger than me – and for the first time in my life I really felt middle aged. Because of the four months out of work, combined with the drastically reduce income, the debts were piling up and it was proving very challenging indeed to make ends meet.

FOUR INTREPID ADVENTURERS - ME, JUM, MEGAN AND TOM

Bangkok to Ben Nevis Backwards!

Most nights, Jum and I would be in bed by 7 p.m. and our once active social life had all but disappeared.

Our lovely son Tom was always cheerful though, and he was growing into a very considerate and likeable young man.

Megan, our Westie, was one of the family and Jum had become so close to this cheeky little dog that they were virtually inseparable.

My biggest regret to this day is not sharing my money worries with Jum much sooner. She had total trust in me and I felt very uneasy whenever she talked about our finances. So one day I decided to finally step up to the plate, and spent a few hours explaining how I had screwed up, and how deeply sorry I was.

We had spent thousands on holidays and would go out at least four or five times a month, but that wasn't the reason for the debts. I had a serious guitar and car addiction that had never gone away, and constantly trading these items in for the latest model had all added up into a huge loss over the last decade or more.

We were facing a financial meltdown, and as I revealed the sheer scale of our deficit I could see my wife's face start to form a frown. Her sad eyes met mine and she was shaking her head.

Oh my God, if I felt bad before, this was one thousand times worse.

I had let Jum down.

I had let Tom down.

I'd even let Megan down.

What a total loser...

We didn't speak for at least an hour, and when she came into the shed, the place where I went when things got bad, I fully expected to get both barrels.

'Phil, what we gonna do?'

Her voice wasn't angry; in fact I could detect a tone that I had never associated with Jum before. I realised it was desperation, with disappointment mixed in.

This was no real surprise, because although I had thought I was shielding my wife from the horrific reality, I'd merely been pulling the wool over her eyes. She was the practical one in the Hall family, and if I had asked her for ideas and help much earlier we would probably not be in this awful mess.

Time for Change?

Even worse, this sharing of bad news had come just after Jum had returned from Thailand, where she had buried her father. Samran was a terrific man who had been very close to his second eldest daughter. Sadly he was diagnosed with liver cancer, and was taken in a few short months. This had coincided with the loss of my well paid job, and although we couldn't afford any expenditure at this sensitive time, Jum had to go and I fully understood this. The rest of her family were less close to my wife and I sensed a real power shift in the Naenudon family, one that we would experience more than once in the future.

'Why you not tell me before I go Thailand?' she said now.

Of course, had I explained our financial issues at that time, she would most definitely not have been able to say goodbye to Samran. I had made the right choice, but at this moment it certainly felt as if I had simply added to a catalogue of rubbish decisions.

We talked for what seemed like hours about the rut we were in, and somewhere during this conversation I started to feel some of the weight lifting off my mind. A problem shared... etc. Sadly, after talking through various scenarios it seemed that no escape route was on offer. Jum was convinced that a visit to the Citizens Advice Bureau was the way forward, and after a week of being reminded, I made the appointment.

The CAB were actually very helpful and showed me how to apply for free financial advice; within a month the Hall family were on a Debt Management Plan. (I would advise anyone reading this to do likewise if you have debt issues. Naturally, better advice would be to never overspend, but it seems that half of the UK is currently in a similar position.)

So this was about two years earlier, if my memory serves me correctly; how does it tie into the house sale, you may be wondering?

Okay, I'll try and make it short and a little sweet.

The debts were slowly being managed and despite my lack of enthusiasm for answering the phone fifty times a day, life on the PepsiCo service desk wasn't so bad. I made some friends, and some of them are still speaking to me to this day!

After a year or so as a Level One Analyst I heard a familiar voice on the other end of the line.

'Hey Phil, what is up?'

It was Manish, one of the two guys I had trained a year earlier. It transpired that the boys from Bangalore had not only taken my job, but now they were grabbing a slice of the service desk action, too.

Instead of feeling annoyed, I was surprisingly happy to hear his dulcet tones.

Sonata, the software company, were now helping out on the service desk, but it seemed things were not going too well.

PepsiCo staff had issues with their call-taking prowess, and the thick South Indian accents were not helping matters. In fact, it was common practice for customers to hang up the phone once they detected that the service desk analyst was not UK-based. This was causing all kinds of problems, and according to our manager things had to change – or else! The standards of Sonata's service desk team had to improve quickly, or PepsiCo would soon be looking elsewhere for assistance.

Why should I care? After all, these were the scoundrels who had contributed to my financial strife – let them rot!

Well, those were my original thoughts, but they were soon replaced with something a lot more practical.

About a year previously I had graduated from The Open University with a degree in English Language Studies. I had then completed a one year TEFL course that equipped me with the skills to teach English as a Foreign Language. In my mind I had hoped that one day, the Hall family could go back to Thailand and I would work as an English teacher., but that seemed to be on the backburner for now, especially considering the quagmire of debt I had forcefully driven us into.

But I could see a sliver of opportunity presenting itself as I thought about the Sonata dilemma. Surely I could use my recently acquired skills to help these guys, and possibly further my own career into the bargain?

So I drew up a little Service Improvement plan that included several key steps, all aimed at making the boys from Bangalore better at their job.

Jo, my manager, was a friendly lady and she seemed fairly interested in my plan. 'Okay Phil, let me share your ideas with the Leadership Team.'

Time for Change?

Great, she had at least listened to me, and if nothing else I had a small chance of success. PepsiCo was a company that prided itself on listening to its employees and encouraged them to come forward with any ideas or schemes that could help improve the way things were done.

Of course, these were simply words, and after a few weeks I had all but forgotten about the plan.

Not so.

I can still remember the morning when Jo asked me to come into the small meeting room, and the surprise I felt when I saw some very senior managers smiling at me as I sat down opposite them.

At first I wondered what I had done wrong. Had I been rude to a customer?

Julie Delargy, the IT director, was there, so something big was about to go down.

'Phil, we have looked at your Service Improvement Plan and we'd like you to go to India!'

Oh my God! Had she actually said those words to me?

Julie went on to explain that the Leadership team had been so impressed with my idea, and that this was the type of proactive plan that they were always on the lookout for. She asked would I like to go?

'Yes, please!'

A few hours later I was at home excitingly telling Jum and Tom about my forthcoming trip to Bangalore. This was the happiest I had felt for a very long time, and the Hall household almost felt good once more. Despite my complete destruction of our funds, maybe this was the glimmer of hope that we needed?

About two weeks later I was in the Emirates Business Class lounge gorging on Champagne and oysters, despite it being only 8 a.m.! I was with Assie and Alun, two senior managers who travelled to India and beyond at least ten times a year. To them, this was probably as exciting as finding out a new dish on the menu of their favorite restaurant. But for me, well, I was making the most of it!

They explained that we would be staying in the Oberoi Hotel in Bangalore, a 5-star residence that sounded sumptuous.

Both of these guys were younger than me and they were

a little curious as to how, at the grand age of 45, I was only a Level One service desk analyst. I explained my working history and told Assie, a South African national, that I had spent six years in his home country. He was a little surprised, and both of them were full of sound advice that I was happy to take on board.

Life is strange! If I had listened to my parents' advice and gone to university back in the day, perhaps I could have been in their shoes.

(Actually, as I found out later, neither of these successful fellows had bothered with further education. So much for that theory!)

The flight was a two-legged affair, and I decided that Business Class had definitely agreed with me. The ten days absolutely flew by, and I was in my element. English language training, plus product knowledge with more than a little fun mixed in, had made the trip a really fulfilling experience. Bangalore was a huge city and despite the hideous traffic I really enjoyed the place, and all that was on offer. We managed to fit in a cricket match, and although I was out for a duck, this was the most fun I had ever had whilst doing my job. My co-workers were a pleasure to train, and when I returned to PepsiCo HQ I was full of enthusiasm.

I tried to find Jo to share my findings with her, but things had changed drastically in a very short time. She had taken on another role and her replacement, Richard Jones, was rather less than impressed with my Indian Odyssey.

He was introduced to me by Gill, the IT Director, and I could feel some fairly negative vibes coming from him. He seemed almost bored as I told them both about the improvements I felt had been made.

As Gill sauntered off to her office, Richard looked at me and said, 'Now, back in the real world...'

I had been brought back down to earth with a bang and started to think about ways to spend as little time as possible with Richard Jones. Despite the wonderful experience and a head full of ambitious plans for the future, it appeared that I would soon be looking elsewhere for any chance of achieving them, if ever!

Over the next few months I was to learn that Mr Jones intended to reshape the service desk, and anybody over the age of 35 had no place in his plans. So I kept my head down

Time for Change?

and was on the constant lookout for new roles, inside and outside of PepsiCo.

After a few failed applications for jobs in different departments I started to realise that my options were limited.

Who wanted to give me, a 45-year-old man, the chance to learn a new trade?

To make matters worse, both Jum and Tom were facing difficulties of their own, at work and school respectively.

The small win that Bangalore had offered was long since forgotten, and the Hall family were on the back foot once more.

I was feeling sorry for myself one Friday afternoon in February 2011, and Manish must have felt bored at work because he called me for a chat.

'Hey bro, how is life?'

His ever-cheerful voice failed to lift me out of the terrible mood I was in, and I decided to make this one of the shortest trans-world telephone conversations in history.

'What do you want Manish?' I asked rather rudely.

'Phil, I was just going to ask about the work schedule for tomorrow…' But he could tell that this was to be brief; and then Manish said eight words that were to change my life forever.

'Why don't you come and work for Sonata?'

'What do you mean?' I was already speculating in my mind about where this may lead.

He explained that Sonata were always interested in taking on new talent, and my reputation was still golden in light of the rescue operation last year.

Later on that evening I ran the idea past Jum and Tom, and although my wife was dead against the very thought of upping sticks and moving to India, Tom was onside almost immediately. He'd had more than his fair share of troubles recently, thanks to some racist idiots hell bent on pointing out the differences between a half-Thai thirteen-year-old and a 100% English equivalent.

Jum herself had also experienced the ugly side of nationalism in her workplace, and the lack of support in both incidents had led me to question why we were even still living in the UK. She agreed to sleep on the idea, and I realised

Bangkok to Ben Nevis Backwards!

that I really was jumping the bloody gun here. I hadn't even approached Sonata officially yet, let alone been interviewed for a position that may not even exist.

My life was full of this type of scenario and always, always, it was down to my lack of patience.

I left for work in the morning about 6.30 am. Both Jum and Tom were fast asleep. On the way to Theale I decided that today was the day for me to approach Sonata for the job that may only be a figment of mine and Manish's imagination.

Three hours later, after at least thirty phone calls, I was on a break and instead of leaving my desk for coffee and biscuits, I plucked up the courage to call Bangalore. I felt that before approaching Jum, I should at least have some agreements in place. I knew that it would possibly cause some serious arguments between us so why risk that if nothing was to come of this?

They were some five and a half hours ahead so I calculated it would be mid-afternoon in the Sonata offices. I dialled Anil's number – he was the project manager and I had got on famously with him during my ten-day jaunt last year.

'Hey Phil, how are you?' His friendly tones were in stark contrast to Richard Jones's.

'Anil, I need to ask you a question please?'

It was now or never...

'Sure, go ahead'

'Is there a job for me at Sonata?' There, I had said it, no going back and all that.

'You want to work for Sonata, Phil?' He sounded a little taken aback, but I also detected a sliver of interest.

'Yes, I really do!' I replied, trying not to sound desperate.

And that was that. About an hour later he called back and, having spoken to the director, Mr Murtthy, Anil confirmed their interest in me working for Sonata Software Ltd. The dream was becoming a distinct reality, and already I was picturing the Hall family in a huge house nestled somewhere in the suburbs of Bangalore.

I supposed I had better mention this to Richard; although facing the other way and on a conference call, he was sat directly in front of me and had the habit of sending me

Time for Change?

emails instead of simply looking up and engaging me in conversation. You see, at this point I had decided that whatever transpired, I absolutely could not work with this cold fish. Richard was a lousy manager and an even worse human being.

So I sent him an email and looked on as he opened and read the electronic message. There was no change in expression and yet again, instead of looking up, he replied within five minutes telling me that he 'didn't think it would be in either PepsiCo's or Sonata's interest'.

Well, we would bloody well see about that!

I went directly to Nigel's office and was pleasantly surprised to see him speaking to both Assie and Alun. Nigel was the Chief Information Officer for PepsiCo UK and he was as senior as you could get within the whole set up.

They were a little shocked when I, a lowly minion, had the temerity to knock on the door – the audacity! Typically, somebody on my pay grade would only have the opportunity to meet Nigel at a corporate event – but I was on a mission and really needed to seal this deal today.

I explained my situation and must have been speaking for about five minutes when I realised all three of these guys were smiling back at me. In short, they agreed that this was a smashing idea and couldn't see why Richard, let alone anyone else, would have a problem with it.

That evening I discussed my potential job offer again with Jum and Tom and they were both in agreement. Possibly a little too easily swayed, I thought, but I wasn't going to ask a second time. Jum's make or break condition was that we brought our lovely Westie, Megan, along for the adventure. Against all odds, it seemed the Hall family were Bangalore-bound!

We placed the house on the market and provided that we got somewhere near the asking price, we should have enough money to start a new life. After a few false starts we received an offer not too short of the mark, and things were moving along swimmingly.

Richard was not exactly enthusiastic, so I dealt mainly with Gill when it came to sorting out the details. Because I was on a low grade it was clear that PepsiCo were not going to dig deep into their pockets to smooth the way, but I tried my best to negotiate a deal that would help us make the move.

One afternoon, Richard emailed me from his desk and requested my presence in approximately one hour. Exactly sixty minutes later he stood up and kind of looked my way; this was as close as he ever got to being friendly.

As we walked towards the cafeteria he looked at me and said, 'I'm really excited about this!'

I could hardly believe my ears! 'Me too,' I replied.

We entered the cafeteria and as we approached the serving hatch he looked like a little kid at Christmas. 'I've been thinking about having a go at these burritos all morning!'

I should have known.

He munched his way through the first fairly vile-looking folded Mexican pancake as I simply sat and waited for His Grace to get to the point of this meeting.

Essentially, although I would be working for a third company service provider, I would still be a conduit between Pepsico and Sonata. In my opinion, I would be offering a valuable service that would benefit both companies. Pepisco often bemoaned the fact that there were no Europeans working for Sonata and apparently they had a lot of plans to offer more work to the Indian IT company. Instead of flying Alun and Assie out up to ten times each per year, I felt as if my own skills could be useful for interviewing potential contractors who would then be working directly with Pepsico on long term contracts.

Indeed, I had made these points, plus a few, more to Gill and Nigel earlier. As a result, I had hoped that my value may be rewarded by my current paymasters.

What seemed like hours later, Richard looked at me through thick frames and let me have it.

'Okay, with regards to your move to India,' he said, rolling his eyes as he mentioned the country. 'We have decided to give you...'

This was the news I was waiting for; would it be flights, hotel, or both, I wondered?

'... nothing!'

There it was: the killer punchline.

His face turned into a sneer and at that moment I could quite cheerfully have shoved the second burrito deep into

Time for Change?

his pasty white face. Jones had waited some time for this opportunity, and boy, was he ever relishing the whole power play.

He went on to say that PepsiCo would pay my salary for the first four weeks at Sonata but only if I continued to man the service desk whilst in this transitional mode.

This was something, and I suppose and I did my best to look and sound pleased, because I knew that any sign of disappointment would make his day.

At this point I hadn't really negotiated my salary with Anil, nor did I actually know what my new role was going to be. All I knew was that I needed to leave the UK and this was my chance, so the details could be sorted out later.

We had spoken to Tom's school and they were happy enough, especially when I explained that India had an IGCSE syllabus and the education system was extremely well thought of. In the UK we have the GCSE syllabus and the Indian version followed the same topics and grading system. It was also transferrable back to the UK as far as credits were concerned.

So the time came when we received a firm offer on the house, and I was starting to believe that this pipe dream was finally happening. The only real problem that I could now see was – what would happen between the time that we moved out of the house and flew onwards to India? I couldn't book tickets or organise visas until we had the equity in the bank, but where would we stay once the house was sold? Things were getting difficult once more and, not for the first time, I had doubts about the whole event.

Then I started thinking about the people we would be leaving behind – especially my parents. I hadn't paid them much thought, to be honest, and although they lived more than 500 miles away, near Fort William, we did our best to visit them three or four times a year.

Mum and Dad were both in their seventies and Dad's health had recently taken a tumble. He was showing early signs of Vascular Dementia, and the more I read about this terrible condition, the more worried I became.

Of course, we would have to go and say goodbye to Mum and Dad, but I hadn't even factored this into the whole equation.

Bangkok to Ben Nevis Backwards!

After making a phone call and giving Mum the news that we were moving to India, she sounded happy, if a little detached. Then she suggested something that appeared to be a solution for our latest quandary.

'Why don't you come and stay with us until the house sale goes through, dear?'

This made perfect sense and, not for the first time, Mum had come up with a rescue plan – the latest in a very long line, I might add!

Mum and Dad had moved up to Roy Bridge about ten years ago and they absolutely loved the place. On a clear day you could see Aonach Mor and Ben Nevis from their front window. Despite the seemingly constant rain, Mum and Dad had chosen a lovely place to spend their retirement years.

Dad had spent some twenty plus years in the services and Mum was a teacher turned author. She had written three books and even had a little fan club as the result of these extremely well received autobiographies.

But I'll talk more about Mum and Dad later, so let's get back to the closing details of Chapter One first!

Instead of putting my plan to Richard I went directly to Gill, and she was happy enough for me to work remotely from Mum and Dad's home until our own house sale went through. I had calculated that this would be in around two weeks' time, and that the remaining two weeks would be sufficient to organise flights and visas for the three of us – and of course Megan.

On my very last day in the Theale offices of PepsiCo I had many desk visitors who all wished me well, and for the first time I realised that I was leaving a fine set of colleagues and a very decent workplace.

Richard had one final hand to play of course, and even though I wasn't surprised, it was a little sad! A colleague had left the service desk a few weeks earlier, and on his last day Richard had organised a presentation. We'd had a whip round and he was given a few nice gifts, plus a card signed by the whole desk and a few others besides.

But as 5 o'clock loomed closer and closer it was pretty apparent that I was going to have no such gesture.

I had asked one of my workmates, Matty, about this

Time for Change?

earlier and he confirmed that Richard had decided not to give me a card and had instructed that nor was anyone else to, because I wasn't really leaving the service desk.

Fair point, but even though I would still be speaking to my former colleagues on a regular basis, I was leaving Pepsico to go and work in another bleedin' continent!

A petty little man to the last!

So at exactly 5 p.m. on September 21st 2011, I logged out of my workstation for the last time and left the building without so much as a by-your-leave.

This slap notwithstanding, as I drove home I soon forgot about the anti-climax and started looking forward to a future with some real potential for once!

Chapter 2

ON OUR WAY

So here we were! The car was fully packed, and 35 Norman Way was soon to be part of the Hall family history. After one last sweep of the house I started up the engine of the Vauxhall hire car and we left Wallingford to begin the next part of our family life: onwards to Roy Bridge and Bangalore, and God knows where else?

As we pulled out of the narrow driveway, the rental car filled to the brim with possessions, humans and a rather small dog, I felt an emotion that had been absent from my life for at least a few years – hope!

Okay, we were taking a huge gamble, of that there could be no doubt, but wasn't that what my life had been all about?

You see, I had trodden the well-worn road for nearly ten years and, despite my best efforts, things had not really worked out.

I read somewhere that we have to work out what is best for us, and that can sometimes take half a lifetime – in fact some people will go from the cradle to the grave and never get anywhere near this discovery.

All I really knew was that this part of our lives was now over, and whatever lay ahead, well – surely it had to be more exciting and promising. The house sale was was nearly through, the drab job had served its purpose, and what lay ahead of the Hall family was already showing signs of promise that life in South Oxfordshire couldn't hope to compare with. So the plans for the next three or four weeks were to prove not exactly a walk in the park, but shouldn't

Bangkok to Ben Nevis Backwards!

prove to be *that* difficult, should they?

In a nut shell, this was the way that I hoped it would go:

1. Spend some time with Mum and Dad;
2. Whilst the sale of the house went through I would build foundations in Bangalore;
3. Once the house had sold and contracts had been exchanged – money in the bank, and all that – we would apply for Indian visas;
4. Then flights would be booked, including Megan's;
5. We would say farewell and fly off in the sunset.

A very sweet plan that made me smile just thinking about it. There were no debts involved, no Richard Jones, and plenty of unknowns that made this adventure something to really look forward to.

As we left the A34 and headed North West on the M40 towards Birmingham I noticed that Jum, Tom and Megan were all fast asleep – in fact, they were snoring in unison. It was still very early, about 5 am, and we had more than 500 miles before we got to Mum and Dad's.

It had been a while since we'd made the trip and I had missed them both very much indeed. The last visit had not ended well, and I thought about this experience as I pointed the car towards the M6 Toll road – which was totally free of traffic, so I floored the accelerator.

Tom and I had decided to pop up to the house and surprise them as they returned from a holiday in the USA.

We got to the house a couple of days before their return and we had a grand old time, fishing in the nearby river and playing all kinds of video games on Tom's X-box. It was the kind of bonding experience that had been sorely lacking from our lives, and I really enjoyed the opportunity to get to know my son a little better.

We had joked about the way the returning travellers would react to our occupation of their home, and I had to admit I was really looking forward to seeing their collective faces. But of course, this type of surprise never quite goes to plan, and we were soon to learn that lesson in spades!

The two days flew by, and we tidied the house up in anticipation. As we pulled up outside the train station, there he was, Colin Raymond Hall, my father. Mum looked absolutely shattered, and Dad had a very odd expression on his face. I embraced Mum and went over to shake his hand, but all I got in return was a very vacant stare.

'Why are you here?' he demanded, and avoided the handshake, ambling towards my car.

He gave Tom a slightly warmer welcome, and we drove the half mile back to Glenspean Park in total silence.

An hour or so later Mum told me about their trip and how stressful it had been; I felt really sad as she regaled me with details of how my father had seemed to totally lose his way during those four weeks.

One of the problems with any form of Dementia is the way that sufferers react to new surroundings. Everything needs to be in place for them, and leaving his familiar home for a bunch of hotels, a strange house and dozens of challenging personal interactions was exactly *not* what the doctor had ordered. I realised that I had seriously underestimated his condition, and was thinking about cutting this visit short when Dad kind of made up my mind for me.

'I want you to go now!' he commanded, and as I looked up, I met a stern pair of eyes looking directly at me.

This was not the reunion I had been picturing but I knew that we should probably leave right away. Mum tried to make us change our minds, but her body language couldn't hide the sheer exhaustion she must be feeling, so we left.

I knew at that moment that Dad would never be the same again, and neither would our extended family.

Part of my heart died that day, and I suppose this is what every child goes through when their heroes start to fade.

Thinking about that whole debacle now did plant a few seeds of doubt in my mind about the next four weeks, but Mum had convinced me that his Dementia had not really grown any worse, and to come.

'What time is it?'

Jum's unusually quiet voice interrupted my less than peaceful thoughts, and as I told her she had been sleeping for three hours I could see that we had just passed Manchester on the M6.

We talked about the whole set of possibilities that lay ahead and I spent most of the time reassuring her about how awesome everything would be. She wasn't convinced, and she reminded me about Dad's car crash some six months earlier. Colin Hall was a very proud and stubborn man, and the onset of Dementia had done nothing to reduce these 'qualities'. His driving license had long since expired, so he certainly wasn't insured any longer. But despite his doctor's advice, Dad had continued to drive at every opportunity, and there was nothing Mum could do to convince him otherwise.

So when I learned of the inevitable car crash, I gritted my teeth and hoped for the best. The roads around Fort William were renowned for accidents and I had images of their tiny hatchback being smashed to smithereens by a tourist bus, or even an eighteen-wheeler truck.

Apparently Mum and Dad were on a weekly shopping trip and Dad was driving; they had finished up and were pulling out onto the busy main road. According to Mum, there was a God Almighty bang and their car was spun around to the point where it was facing the other way.

As the driver of the other car got out and made his way over to my parents he was rather shocked to see my Dad picking up cans and bottles from the road. Mum was still reeling from the accident and there was Dad, more bothered about his bloody groceries!

Of course that was not the case. My Dad was not well, and should have never been behind the wheel of that car. I still have bad feelings when I think of the possible alternative outcome.

By the time I had played these memories through my mind the entire Hall family Robinson had awoken, and I decided we'd stop at the very next services.

Jum walked and watered Megan as Tom and I were put on sandwich duty. As we walked towards the Carlisle services he started asking me about the road ahead – not the M6, but the rather bigger picture.

This was the first time I had noticed any type of concern in his questions, and I did my best to calm this remarkable young man.

'What happens if the house doesn't sell?'
'What if my new school is rubbish?'
'Will Granddad even recognise us?'
'What type of food will we eat on the plane?'

I managed to come up with a measured response to this

On Our Way

line of interrogation and we chose a few overpriced rolls to chow down on in the car.

About fifty minutes later we crossed the border to my homeland. I looked back in the rear view mirror and said a tentative goodbye to England.

'When will we see Ben Nevis, Dad?'

Tom had fallen in love with Scotland and her breathtaking scenery the first time they had been introduced a decade earlier. He had asked Mum where she was moving to, as she and Dad broke the news in their Bristol Home just before the new millennium had broken.

'Well dear, our new home will be just behind Ben Nevis and not too far from the Loch Ness monster.' She said this with a twinkle in her eyes, but all Tom had taken in was a single word.

'Monster?'

Tom's eyes had doubled in size, and his grandmother spent the next hour regaling him with stories of Nessie; a bond began to form that exists to this very day.

I had hoped that Mum and Dad would have seen far more of Tom in the past – and even the future – but that five-hundred-mile-plus road was a killer and had a serious impact on the frequency of our visits.

I was as always taken aback by the sheer beauty of the Scottish countryside, especially as we swept past Glasgow and headed towards Perth. Such a stunning backdrop, with some beautiful Big Sky action going down! This seemed a fitting way to bade farewell to the UK for... who knows how long?

We limited our stops to one every two hours, and by around 6 o'clock we were cruising into Lochaber, with Roy Bridge less than thirty minutes away. Our final stop was in Fort William, and I nipped into the Morrisons as Jum, Tom and Megan had a little walk on the shores of Loch Linne.

To say that my mind was full would be an understatement as I juggled with both emotions and logic, to the point where I had to stop looking for whatever it was and found myself in the frozen food aisle. This was far more difficult than I had imagined, and if I was having doubts already, what use would I be when real judgement and reasoning were the order of the day?

At this moment in time, we were dependent on the house

STUNNING BEN NEVIS

sale completing. If that fell through, what the hell would happen next? I had not thought this through, but the sheer agony of living in that house waiting for the news had proved almost too much to bear.

I had high hopes pinned on the next four weeks being just what we needed, so I gathered the rest of the shopping list and headed towards the check-out.

Just before 7 p.m. we arrived at Glenspean Park, and the mountains were all on show.

'Dad, which one's Ben Nevis?'

To this day I'm not really sure, but they all looked equally breathtaking.

We spilled out of the rental car and I felt such relief when I saw my mother waving at us from the front door.

As we hugged and started to unpack the car, I almost asked where Jocky Boy was. Then I remembered that the grand old Westie had been taken from us at the age of thirteen years. He and Dad were inseparable, and I had wondered what type of negative reaction this may cause, particularly considering Dad's illness. Now, Dad was nowhere to be seen and Mum told me that he was watching

On Our Way

TV. This was no surprise to me, and I made my way towards the lounge through the long narrow corridor.

There he was, sat in his usual chair and giving 100% concentration to *Old Dogs, New Tricks.*

'Hey Dad!'

I was about to ask how he was when he shot me a look that warned me to stop talking – or something along those lines. I waited a few minutes, then decided to go back to the car, and unpacked with Jum and Tom.

It was at least 8 p.m. before the car was finally bereft of our possessions, and I noticed then that Mum hadn't laid on her usual spread. In fact she looked absolutely drained, so I made us both a cup of tea and we had a long overdue chat.

I felt more like a priest listening to a confession than a concerned son, as Mum started talking about life in Roy Bridge since my last visit. Plenty had happened, and most of it was not good news.

After my last visit with Tom had been cut short I had been reluctant to return, and had even kept telephone contact to the minimum. You see, the way that I usually lived my life was tagged by a well-worn Buddhist phrase: *We don't see life the way it is; we see it the way that we are.* So if Phil Hall was having a crappy day, week, or even year, then surely the whole world was in a similar state. This was part of the reason I so desperately needed to up sticks for pastures new.

'Why India, Phil?'

Not for the first time, my choice of emigration destination was being questioned. Mum's other children were now living in USA, a place that I had visited but never really connected with. To me, India was exciting and mysterious, and it was the first and probably last place where I would be offered a job of any consequence.

As she began to ask more questions I could see where this line of enquiry was going. She was concerned about Tom – or should I say, Tom's education. Quite rightly so, because Mum had been a school teacher for more than three decades and in her opinion, the British education system was the best in the world. However, there was no point in arguing because we were going – and that was that!

I popped into the lounge and Dad was still watching *Old*

Bangkok to Ben Nevis Backwards!

Dogs. In fact, it was the same episode as before! Mum had updated me on his condition and I was starting to worry about how she would manage – I was going to say 'after I was gone', but she had managed without me so far!

'Oh, I'll be alright,' she said in her typically stoic style when I asked her if she would be able to cope with Dad's illness. But I knew that this was simply a brave front and, not for the first time, I realised how strong Mum really was.

This child of South Uist had beaten the odds on more than one occasion, but although I admired her strength of character, this would surely be the hardest battle that Christina Hall would ever face.

As I mentioned previously, Mum was not only a retired schoolteacher and world traveller, she was also a published author. She had written three very well received books, and was going for number four when she was diagnosed as suffering from an aneurism. In actual fact, the sight in her left eye was now almost non-existent, such was the progression of the swollen blood vessel.

The whole event was made even worse by the fact that her English GP had dismissed the potentially lethal condition as old age and nothing else. Thankfully his Fort William counterpart was far more concerned about why Mum had been suffering from head-splitting headaches and loss of sight, so when she correctly diagnosed her with the brain aneurism, we all felt terrible for being a little less concerned than we should have been.

The surgeon told us that Mum had a fifty-fifty chance of surviving the operation and, God Bless her, she beat those odds with ease. There was to be no more book writing, but that didn't stop Mum from enjoying the fan mail that beat a steady trail to her door.

But today, on this rather grey and overcast September morning, I could see how vulnerable she had become – and now she was expected to be a rock once more.

In my mind, I had played over the possibilities available to me many times. For instance, what if when we sold the house we moved up to Roy Bridge instead of Bangalore?

But this idea was soon dismissed by Mum as she explained that the lack of well paid jobs was one of the reasons my brother couldn't wait to leave Lochaber. Instead, she told me to 'follow my dreams' because one day, it could be me sat at the same table wondering why I hadn't taken her sage advice.

I spent the rest of the evening with my father and felt incredible sadness as I observed him going through a strange ritual that included laying down several tissues on the side of his armchair and repeatedly straightening them one by one.

Dad was once a heavy smoker; he was now on roll-ups and seemed to keep losing either the tobacco or papers, or both. More than once during our four-week stay I was confronted by an angry but confused-looking man, demanding what I had done with his 'bloody tobacco papers?'

Our first week in Glenspean Park passed uneventfully and I was trying my best to do my support role from one of the bedrooms with a company laptop and headset. Richard was on my case almost every day, and with each incoming phone call I prayed it was news of the house sale.

Stress started to play a part, and although Jum had told me that Dad had been rather unpleasant to her on more than one occasion, I tried to play this down – until one afternoon I had to get involved.

My wife was always trying to help, and despite my own advice to the contrary, she would always work to keep the house as tidy as possible, even when her help was clearly not appreciated. I was trying in vain to get enthusiastic about taking helpdesk calls one afternoon when I became aware of some kind of kerfuffle going on elsewhere in the house.

When I signed off to go and investigate I found my father and my wife locking horns in the lounge.

'You stupid girl, get out of my house!'

I could tell that this particular meeting of minds had got to the point where something had to give, so I decided to escort Jum out of the room and back into the relative safety of our temporary bedroom.

She was in tears and as she explained that all she was trying to do was tidy up the newspapers that were strewn on the floor, I could tell that there was more to this than she was letting on.

Apparently Dad had been saying unkind things to Jum for at least two weeks – pretty much since we had arrived. He seemed to think that she was some kind of interfering foreign home help, and clearly had no time for this kind young lady. I did wonder if his Dementia had brought him back to the army days of Malaysia and Singapore, when we had a number of local girls working as nannies and housekeepers... but either way, it was clear that the strain of the impending move and living in this smoke-filled, difficult house was taking its toll on Jum.

I kicked myself for not noticing, and even more for thinking this period of our lives would be plain sailing. It most certainly was anything but, and when she asked me what would happen if the house sale fell through... well, I decided that we needed to go for a long walk, and went to find my son.

Tom was locked into his Xbox 360 as usual, and another real worry entered my preoccupied mind. This thirteen-year-old boy had been out of school for nearly two weeks, and I had no real idea of when he would next enter formal education.

What kind of father was I turning out to be?

Not for the first time, my grand master plan was starting to look a little shaky – and we hadn't even booked the flights to India yet.

We were just about to leave the house for a serious walk and talk when a small van pulled up outside the gate. Megan must have sensed something, because she started barking as if her life depended on it. A middle-aged couple emerged, and the lady was holding what appeared to be a very small toy dog – except this was no toy, it was a puppy, and very much alive!

'Mr Hall?' the man enquired, and I responded with a bemused grin and a nod of my head. 'This is your new Westie!'

That was all well and good, but I already had a Westie and certainly wasn't in the mood for one more, especially considering our impending emigration plans, such as they were!

But the little ball of fluff had already worked its way free from the lady's grip and had rushed up to check us out, particularly Megan. He (or she) was adorable, and before I could get close enough, Tom had scooped the tiny pup up in his arms and was tickling his belly.

'Ah, so Jock 2 has arrived then!' Mum was coming down

On Our Way

the garden path far more quickly than I had seen her do before. She explained that this was to be the original Jock's replacement, and she had kept his arrival a secret from Dad.

It was a secret she had also forgotten to share with us, and I was just about to question her motives when Dad's voice rang out behind us.

'Who are these people? Tell them to bugger off!'

He was preparing for a second barrage when Tom presented him with Jock, or at least Jock 2. Dad's expression changed from a frown into a huge smile and for a minute, even Megan stopped barking. The transformation was incredible – God only knows what he was thinking at that moment!

He had been so downcast after Jock died that for a time Mum thought he would never speak again; the Dementia hadn't helped matters, and even the doctor was concerned about his frame of mind. I suppose Mum had been clutching at straws, but the replacement seemed to already be having a positive effect on this very ill man, and for that I applauded her!

Jock 2 was only three months old but had more than his fair share of beans, and was scared of nobody and nothing. Our family walk eventually went ahead, and my head was spinning by the time we left the house.

'Okay guys, how do you think it's going so far?' I asked, almost afraid of the answers.

Tom was his usual self and seemed to think we were having a splendid old time, no worries there. But Jum was not happy, and with very good reason.

'Phil, I cannot stay in the house when your Dad is nasty to me.'

Although I could well understand her stance, surely she could understand that my father was not a well man?

'No Phil, your Dad and Mum have never liked me.'

This was a bit harsh I thought, though there had been times since our marriage that both of my parents had seemed a little distant to Jum.

I tried to play it down. 'Listen, we only have two or three weeks left; please can we just keep our heads down?'

'What happens if the house doesn't sell? What will we do then?'

Of course, I couldn't bear to think of that happening.

The debts, the job, our whole bloody future would be up in smoke.

'It will sell, we are nearly there, please darling...'

My words trailed off, because in the distance I saw a sight that will stay with me for the rest of my days. I had to look again to be sure of what I was witnessing.

An elderly man was struggling with what appeared to be a white banshee on the end of a rope. Dad was taking the three month old Jock 2 out for a walk. He was too young – Jock 2, that is – and probably needed some injections before it was safe foir him to be out of the house!

I tried to convince Dad to do an about turn and return home, but of course that was far easier said than done. Colin Raymond Hall was nothing if not a determined man, and even after succumbing to Vascular Dementia, if he intended to do something, nobody had better get in his way. Twenty-odd years in the army and a cast iron will had moulded this chap into a pretty successful person, and although we never really became that close, I will always respect my father for what he'd achieved.

His own father had left his family when Dad was a small boy, and in those days a divorce was nothing short of scandalous. The lack of a father figure had made it difficult for Dad to relate to any type of role model, but in my opinion he had done okay.

My mind went back to our South African days and I smiled as I remembered him building a small yacht from a flat-pack kit. Buying and assembling the yacht from scratch cost about a quarter of the price of a finished article. Dad had spent nearly a year in the garage assimilating the boat's plans and painstakingly putting it together. This included a good deal of drilling, sawing and, eventually, varnishing and painting. The whole family was amazed when he called us out to the swimming pool area where we witnessed this beautiful yellow Mirror dinghy floating away happily in the sunlight.

I couldn't even dream of achieving such an objective, and to this day I'm still pretty awestruck by the whole process.

Within a few weeks we had joined the local yacht club and each of the children took it in turns to crew as Dad skippered us on to victory – or at least, that was the plan. He had painted the name *Brae Lynne* onto the boat and this made me smile, even now, for it was the name of Mum's home back in Kilpheder, South Uist.

Speaking of Mum, she never ever went on the little yacht because despite having being born and brought up on an island, she couldn't swim. Myself, well, swimming was no problem but I hated being on *Brae Lynne,* thanks to a particular race that we entered.

Benoni sailing club used an old reservoir for all of its scheduled races, and sometimes the water was a little choppy, due to its particular design.

One Sunday afternoon it was my turn to crew, and as I pulled on my bright yellow lifejacket I involuntarily shuddered, looking up at the black sky and feeling the rain start to fall from the heavens.

They certainly opened that afternoon, but after a tentative start to the race we had somehow picked up a bucketful of wind and, for once, we were actually leading the pack! In fact, for about thirty seconds I totally forgot the rancid weather conditions and was throwing all of my eleven-year-old body and mind into this event.

As I leaned over the side of the boat to counteract the fierce winds I started to realise that my own lack of weight was soon going to come into play. Myself and Dad had strapped our feet into the belts fixed to the side of the Mirror, and I had never seen Dad's face look so happy before – or since, for that matter.

But our joy was to be short lived, as the entire boat flipped over and I found myself wrapped around the spinnaker and swimming for my life just ten seconds after our finest moment.

Righting a small yacht was no mean feat, and the process involved the crew adding their weight to the centreboard until the boat was back on an even keel, so to speak. Our combined weight was probably only around ninety kilograms, and as we battled to get *Brae Lynn* ready for action, the entire Benoni yacht club smirked as they sailed past.

By the time we had managed the task in hand we had been lapped at least four times, and Dad decided to withdraw due to 'technical reasons'. Dad didn't even ask me whether I was okay or not, and I never crewed again after that day. Pride is a powerful emotion, and I'm not sure if that event actually harmed our relationship, but it definitely did nothing to strengthen the bond between father and son.

Bangkok to Ben Nevis Backwards!

So - fast forward some thirty-five-odd years and it seemed as if the roles had reversed, as I was now trying to convince this mentally ill man to return to his home with the tiny puppy in tow. I cursed my own luck, and really could have done without this drama adding to my own distress.

We eventually managed to turn him around, and after drying off I remembered that I had been away from the PepsiCo phones for over two hours without letting Richard know my intentions. My work mobile had six missed calls and three text messages.

'Where the hell have you been?'

I tried to explain my fraught afternoon to Richard, to no avail, and although his lack of empathy was no surprise, I was really starting to hate this man.

Richard was a results-driven character and had no time for drama, or even personal interactions. I found him to be a divisive chap who clearly played favourites, and seemed to think nothing of verbally laying into his staff whilst other departments were within earshot. I had never really been a manager but if that day ever came, I certainly knew that this was not the route that I would follow.

'Phil, I can't stay here.' Jum's soft voice interrupted my fantasy of dunking Richard into a swimming pool of Pepsi Cola via an eighteenth century witch's ducking stool. But Jones would have to wait for now, because my wife needed my attention more than ever.

She went on to tell me about how she had tried to help Dad with Jock 2 shortly after we got back from the walk, and how he had told her to 'get out!' of the house.

I tried to explain that this was no longer my father, the illness had replaced his reasoning, but she had already made up her mind. We had to leave.

So to add to the already considerable challenges before us, my wife was now throwing a huge spanner in the works.

I was considering my options when my mobile started to ring, and I pretty much lost my cool. Richard's name lit up on the screen, and I decided to simply switch the phone off.

I put on my shoes, left the house and climbed into the hire car. We were supposed to return this car the next day, but I needed to be alone and, after checking that I had the

On Our Way

documents with me, I began driving to Inverness alone.

As plans go, mine were pretty much in the toilet by now.

I had predicted that the house sale would have been completed by now, and after returning the car we would have a weekend in Inverness and do some shopping for our Asian adventure. We'd also spend a night in a decent hotel and do our best to paint the Scottish town red.

But that hadn't happened. Pretty much every single possible obstacle had come into play and at this moment in time, I really couldn't see anything working out in our favour.

As I negotiated the car onto the Inverness road, I ran through the possible options in my confused and angry mind:

- I could do my best to keep things as they were and hope Jum would change her mind – not likely!
- Look for a nearby bed and breakfast, and hopefully she would return in a few days.
- Have it out with Mum and Dad and get him to apologise – more chance of winning the lottery.

Then it struck me: these were all little things in comparison to the house sale, the move to India, the new Job, Tom's new school...

It wasn't going to happen.

I could see now that my planning had been both selfish and rash. I had taken my son away from a school that he loved, and my wife from the life she had loved in Wallingford. Despite the downsides they'd experienced, they were content to be where they were.

Phil Hall, not for the first time, had misread the situation and, thanks to his own pretty rubbish view on life, had decided to turn the whole thing upside down for the first escape route that had appeared.

I stopped the car at the Commando War Memorial just outside Spean Bridge and switched off the radio for some serious rethinking.

If I had learned anything in my forty-five years on this planet, I knew that any plan could be changed. Nothing was set in stone. Also, I did understand that family must come first. It had taken nearly fourteen years of married life, but I

Bangkok to Ben Nevis Backwards!

had finally got that fact, and now I needed to make another choice based on current circumstances.

I closed my eyes and for about ten or maybe fifteen minutes thought about how we could get past this. I was worried about Mum and Dad – how would they manage after we had left? All of their offspring would be at least three thousand miles away, and who knows what would happen next with Dad's condition?

I also worried about my wife and son. What kind of a man was I to lead them down this route without a solid backup plan?

I remembered Anil's words of wisdom the last time we spoke: 'Phil, you should have a Plan B just in case things do not go as well as you would like them to.'

Hell, I hadn't even booked the bloody flights yet, and the wheels had all but come off the whole shebang!

Perhaps I could return to PepsiCo with my tail between my legs and see if the almighty Mr Jones could see his way to let me re-join the team? To be honest I couldn't really see that happening; I had heard through the grapevine that they were already interviewing victims for my job. But anything had to be better than where we were right at this moment...

And then the phone rang.

'Phil, the contracts have been exchanged! Your house has been sold!'

In an instant everything changed in my world; hope was banging on the door.

I couldn't muster much in the way of a reply, but as I turned the car around and headed back to Roy Bridge, I started smiling like an idiot. A considerable weight had lifted from my shoulders. Perhaps everything was going to be okay after all?

Little did I know...

Chapter 3

SAYING GOODBYE... FOR THE LAST TIME?

Excited that it was all working out at last, I rushed into the house looking for Jum. She was nowhere to be found.

'She's gone dear.'

I looked at my mother and knew something bad had just happened.

My father had told her to leave one time too many, and this time my wife had decided to follow his orders.

'But where could she go?' I asked nobody in particular.

I went to find Tom, who was unexpectedly delighted that the house sale had gone through, and we set off together to find Jum. It didn't take too long; my phone rang and I could see her name flash up on my screen. She'd checked herself into the local B&B and was waiting in the front garden with Megan as we approached.

'I can't stay there Phil, your Dad hates me too much,' she said tearfully as soon as I reached her.

'It's okay darling, we've sold the house!'

I tried to reassure her but my good news had little effect on her sad face.

'I don't want to go to India Phil; can't we go back to Wallingford?'

Jesus, I thought, why is she being so difficult? I got the fact that she was upset at the way my mentally-ill father had spoken to her; we'd all had a dose of his vitriol, but for Pete's sake!

'Mum, come on, we can leave soon and start our new life!'

At least Tom was on my side, even though he didn't have a full grasp of what was going on. Okay, he knew that we were waiting for the house to sell before we moved to India, but as for Dad's condition and the fragile state of affairs between me and Jum, well, that hadn't really held a candle to the fun he'd been having with his online computer games. He'd kept his head down since we'd arrived, and that was probably a good idea.

After staying quiet for at least 5 minutes, Jum looked up, held my hand and stared right into my eyes. 'Phil, do you realise today is your Happy Birthday?'

Jum always referred to it this way and she was right, it was October 7th 2011 and I was officially an old fart at 46 years old – and today was the day the house sale was completed! I wasn't one for celebrating birthdays, least of all my own, but I usually could at least acknowledge the fact. Perhaps this was what old age was about, and I too had started the steady roll into some form of dementia?

I laughed and demanded to know where my cards and presents were, but there were none. We'd been so wrapped up in the bloody house sale and Dad's dementia that my birthday had slipped everyone's mind, including mine. After all, it was hardly a milestone.

The only present that I truly wanted at that moment was to be magically transported some five thousand miles East of here, with everything in place. But I realised that before any of that could happen, some serious bridge-building needed to be done and plenty of red tape needed cutting.

Jum invited us inside and the B&B owner offered us a cup of tea. He was a kind chap who knew Mum and Dad had seen better days, and he sympathised fully with our dilemma. His own parents had succumbed to Dementia and he understood what we were going through.

I understood that for now, Jum needed some space and after a big group hug, myself and Tom said goodbye to her and Megan, and we returned to Glenspean Park with somewhat mixed feelings. I was overjoyed that the millstone of debt was starting to look as if it would soon disappear, but I still had to try to make peace between my wife and my ill father.

As usual, I had a list of objectives:

Saying goodbye... for the last time?

1. Wait for the money to be transferred to our accounts from the house sale – this would take a little while, possibly up to two weeks... it would feel a lot longer!
2. Once the money was there, book flights for ourselves and Megan;
3. Get tourist visas for Jum and Tom;
4. Look into schools for Tom... something I'd really fallen behind on so far;
5. Pay our final bills for mobile phone accounts, gas and electric, and any other utility bills... this wouldn't be cheap;
6. Speak to our bank about the best way to ensure we always had access to cash abroad.

All this while I doing my 9-5 job of taking calls for Uncle Richard, and somehow making our stay bearable, without too many upheavals.

I also needed to get my wife back onside.

As we approached my parents' house I could see Dad 'walking' Jock 2; the little puppy was doing his level best to escape the oversized collar and lead. Dad literally marched passed us without a hint of recognition, and this time I just didn't have the energy to raise a single objection.

I told Mum that the house sale had gone through, and for the first time in weeks I saw her old smile return. What must she have been going through?

'Is Jum okay?' she asked,

I did my best to make light of it, but she could tell that things weren't good.

'Your father, he doesn't mean those nasty things...'

She looked off into the distance sadly, so I gave her a big hug and reminded my mother that today was the anniversary of the day she'd brought me into this wicked old world.

'Of course it is. Happy Birthday, dear!' and she produced a card with a bunch of twenty pound notes inside.

Wow, she'd remembered even though I hadn't!

We hugged, I thanked her, and we both knew it was for more than just the money.

Then I went to my room and, for the first time in ages, I slept for a good nine hours straight.

Bangkok to Ben Nevis Backwards!

It took me a few days to convince Jum to return, but then things started to move swiftly along. I did have a minor nightmare when trying to book Megan's flight to Bangalore, thanks to a less than helpful operator; essentially the problem was that our plane would stop over in Dubai for a few hours, and even though I had all of the necessary shots and certificates, because I didn't have a permit for her to enter the UAE airspace, she would be refused entry onto the plane.

I only found this out a week or so before we were due to fly, out and I flipped my lid with the airline. Just imagine if we'd arrived at the airport with Megan in tow and had not been able to check her in? The worst case scenario would be missing the flight, and expensive hotel bills – not to mention paying for another three tickets, plus her new flight on top!

The airline apologised but wouldn't budge.

I decided to look into paying for a pet export agency to help, and discovered this was a good idea. After speaking to several, I decided to go with a Falkirk-based company who seemed to know what they were doing.

The costs were fairly high – instead of £100 for Megan's ticket it would be closer to £1000, plus the Indian import charges. But that didn't matter, because at least I could tick this goal off the list. This may come across as a tad cold, but anyone who has been through a move overseas with their pet will know exactly how I felt.

I still had my business visa from the trip with PepsiCo last year, and getting tourist visas for Tom and Jum was easy enough. Before we knew it, we were only a few days away from our exit. I hired a car and we drove up to Inverness to buy some slick new luggage, and we all splashed out on some decent clothes. This was the happiest we'd been for a long time, and I was looking forward to the evening meal out that Mum had promised when we got back.

We'd usually have gone to the Stronlossit Hotel for steaks, but this time Mum wanted us to go somewhere altogether different. Yes, we were about to sample the Little Chef experience! Apparently Dad had taken a liking to the service and food that the chain restaurant had to offer, and I was game for a laugh!

Okay, I had probably become a bit of a food snob over the

Saying goodbye... for the last time?

years, but when we entered the establishment, all dressed up to the nines, I was in for a shock. I'd remembered Heston Blumenthal's program in which he'd tried to breathe life into this rather tired business, but he had obviously overlooked this particular branch.

The staff looked less than impressed at our arrival, and we were forced to find a table ourselves. By the time the waitress finally graced us with her presence, I was about to suggest that we went elsewhere, but I remained calm.

We had one menu between five people, and as Dad stared blankly at the dog-eared document, I could sense the impatience building in the fifty-something lady standing by our table. After one minute she announced that she would be back in ten minutes, and promptly returned to her conversation with another employee.

Jum was the first to complain. She called the server back and asked her why she was being so rude?

'I don't have all day to wait for youse to order.'

This was like showing the proverbial red rag to the bull, and Jum let this miserable wench have both barrels.

Suddenly Dad perked up and joined in, but instead of backing my wife up, he started ripping into Jum. As if this wasn't bad enough, Mum piped up and added insult to injury. I tried to explain that Jum was standing up for *them*, but my parents were having none of it.

The waitress was enjoying the floor show; at least she was until I told her in a few choice words to vacate the scene.

Tom, Jum and I stood up and stormed out of that ridiculous so-called 'restaurant', swearing never to return (we've never frequented one since, and never will). After waiting about five minutes in the hire car, we were joined by Mum and Dad. They were fuming, and we had to endure several minutes of insults, mostly directed towards Jum.

I turned towards Dad and warned him to stop.

'Do you want a problem? Do you?' he replied, and leered at me. For one second I was sorely tempted to let him have it. But I knew that this was not my father – not any more.

We drove straight back to the house and after Tom and Jum left the car, I drove my parents to the Stronlossit for their usual steak dinner.

Back at the house we packed our bags ready for the

morning's journey, and then I returned to the hotel to pick up my confused, yet well fed, parents.

They seemed happy enough, and as I thought about the embarrassing scenes just a few hours earlier I also considered the wonderful meals that we'd shared in some lovely restaurants in both hemispheres. It helped calm me.

Dad went straight to bed and I was just about to retire when Mum asked me if I'd like a drink before the big trip tomorrow. To be honest I would have preferred just to slope off to my room, but there was something in her voice that made me stay.

As she poured me a generous helping of malt whisky she asked me about how I was feeling, so over the next hour or two I told her exactly what I thought. My doubts, my fears... and these were just about leaving her and Dad behind.

As we sank a few drams and relaxed, she did her level best to reassure me that they would be fine. 'Don't you worry about us dear, I'll look after your Dad and we'll be fine.'

She seemed more concerned about my little brood and our impending jaunt than her own, far more considerable, issues, and it was then that I realised I shared this trait with my mother. I'd always downplayed my own problems, even when I was the main cause of them. This was probably not a great blessing and could be the reason for my recent debt issues, but it wouldn't be fair to lay the genetic blame at her feet, especially now.

'Philip, I want you to have this.' Mum passed a cheque into my hand and I could see it was for £5,000.

I hugged my Mum and promised her that I'd look after my family as long as she promised to look after herself and Dad. We had a few more drams and called it a night, as I worried about the level of my impending hangover, especially as I was due to wake up less than four hours later.

As I sunk into the bed I realised that my wedding band was missing! Well, it would have to wait till morning before I'd hunt it down... hopefully.

Daybreak came soon enough and although I didn't feel great, the excitement of the journey dulled my hangover, and while Mum and Dad slept we were buzzing around as we packed our worldly belongings into the hire car. I did

Saying goodbye... for the last time?

leave a few guitars behind, and all our photo albums, plus a few ornaments that we'd not had the heart to throw away. Megan was constantly under our feet, and I wondered how long it would be before we saw her wagging tail once more.

After just thirty minutes we were packed, and I could sense that Jum was uber-keen to get in the car and go. I could hardly blame her. It took a while to wake my parents and I started to think about these dear people that I was leaving – perhaps for the last time.

Dad couldn't even recognise me now, so I guessed he wouldn't miss me, but Mum looked pretty upset as I hugged them both goodbye.

I looked back and could hear Jock 2's shrieking bark as I walked towards the hire car. Although it was barely October, the Lochaber air was cold enough to warrant wearing a jacket, and I'd done exactly that.

As we pulled out of the driveway I was surprised to feel so bloody sad – after all, weren't we doing what the Halls do best? We were leaving the country to start a new life; I could only hope that this would be a better one.

We drove first to Falkirk to take Megan to the pet export people, who had a large kennels set up for their furry flyers. Jum shed a tear or twenty as we bade Megan a warm farewell; she'd only been with us for just four years but had become a huge part of our lives.

An hour later we checked into the Airport Holiday Inn and did a mini-unpack in the comfortable, yet sterile, hotel room. Our flight was the next morning at about 11 o'clock, so we chilled out for a while before going into Glasgow to speak to NatWest bank about our financial arrangements abroad. Once that was done I suggested we have an evening meal back at the hotel, and was slightly dismayed to find that three steak dinners and a few beverages came to nearly £100... another good reason to move to India!

chapter 4

GOOD MORNING INDIA

As our plane touched down in Bangalore I squeezed Jum's hand, as we always did when landing. I tried to grab Tom's but it appeared that he had already outgrown this family custom and was far more interested in what was going on outside.

'Dad, does India have the internet?'

I was somewhat taken aback by this question but smiled inwardly as I thought about how naive I had been all those years ago when the Hall Family Version 1.0 had docked in Cape Town. Okay, Tom was a few years older than I had been back then, but I was looking forward to seeing how my son would develop in this fascinating country.

Just twenty-four hours ago we'd said our tearful goodbyes to Mum and Dad, and here we were, finally ready to take the first steps into a whole new life.

Jum suddenly looked at me quizzically and asked where my wedding ring was? Damn – I'd forgotten to look for it on waking! I explained that I'd somehow misplaced it whilst having a farewell drink with Mum back in Roy Bridge. Instead of expanding on this rather shaky ground I swiftly changed the subject, and started talking about how we were about to embark on a whole new adventure.

I'd lost a few wedding bands before and I had a feeling that Jum would soon be back on this somewhat shaky topic.

We breezed through passport control, and while Jum and Tom waited at the luggage carousel I went to the

Bangkok to Ben Nevis Backwards!

bathroom to try and freshen up.

The last time I'd been here, things were a little less intense. I had been on a 'jolly' and was looking forward to enjoying some quality treatment as well as a bit of challenging work-related tasks.

As I washed my face I looked in the mirror, and saw a bald, middle-aged man staring back at me. He looked a little lost, and pretty much out of his depth. I paused for thought. Here I was, trying to start a new life with my family, in India, of all places! Even the airport bathroom had the smell of an exotic country, and I don't mean that in a bad way.

The attendant started massaging my neck and shoulders, and whilst I would usually have asked him to stop, right now it felt amazing. I kind of drifted off a little, but my mind was still turning over the immense set of objectives I had set for myself.

Okay, there was a promise of a job – heck, I even had a letter, and a few emails to boot. But there were no concrete figures, neither was there an exact job description. In all honesty, I had run so fast from that potential nightmare of debts and uncertainty that I'd literally flown straight into something even more risky.

'You okay sir?'

I snapped out of the funky day dream and tipped the attendant with some leftover Rupees from my last visit.

We were soon past customs and motoring towards Bangalore city centre. The time we'd spent in Roy Bridge was nothing short of horrific, and at that moment I made a promise to myself to live for the moment. At forty-six I was no spring chicken, but I figured that I had another twenty years of functionality left. I decided to dedicate the next two decades to exploring life, and I intended to spend as much time with my two lovely travelling partners as possible.

Before I ended up in a care home, or worse...

Almost exactly one hour later we had arrived outside The Presidential Hotel in the downtown area of the city and were ushered inside by several well-dressed commissars.

'Welcome to the Presidential Hotel, Mr Hall!'

I was both surprised and impressed that our arrival had

been given such a warm reception, and as I filled in the arrival forms I noticed that Tom was getting plenty of attention from the female hotel staff.

'Oh he's so cute!'

'He looks like Justin Bieber!'

Tom was already a good-looking lad and was starting to realise that his face could open doors. Although he was still a few inches shorter than me, I had hoped that he would eventually tower over my own rather limited frame. But he looked more embarrassed right now, so I played on this fact and teased him a little as our lift powered us up to the 5th floor.

We literally crashed out onto the two beds, and Jum was fast asleep before my weary noggin had even made contact with the huge pillows.

What seemed like just minutes later – but was actually about three hours – I awoke to hear some raised voices speaking rapid Hindi in the next room. Jum and Tom were still snoring for Britain, so I tried to unpack quietly and ran the bath as I came to terms with where we were.

India...

This is something that I had looked forward to, even before I had decided to steer my family east. Thanks to Mum and Dad, I had lived in quite a few interesting countries whilst growing up. Yet despite my desire to keep travelling, I had spent 60% of my life in the UK.

America was okay, but didn't really interest me that much. India was the real deal. But was I really prepared for what lay ahead? Were any of us?

Jum had been very quiet since we'd arrived – too quiet. In fact, the only noises that I had heard from her were related to her beloved Megan. She missed the dog so much that I wondered if I'd slipped even further down the pecking order. Before we were blessed with Tom, Jum had pretty much waited on me hand and foot.

Okay, that sounds terrible but it was the truth. You see, in Thailand, or at least in the countryside, husbands are treated like movie stars by their wives. After living alone through my twenties, I had quickly started to enjoy the breakfast-in-bed and feet-washing shenanigans rather a lot.

But it was to be short lived, like most things that seem

too good to be true. Jum fell pregnant with Tom about three months after we exchanged vows, and the foot massages and breakfast duties soon became mine. I loved the bones off my son, but once he popped out I wasn't the numero uno any longer. I supposed most married men have a similar tale to tell.

How unhappy was Jum, really? I had thought the fact that Thailand was only two hours away would be a major selling point, but she'd seemed unimpressed by this. On the other hand, I'd also pointed out that she'd be unable to work in India, which hadn't gone down well. It's fairly hard for Europeans to obtain a work visa there, and even harder for an Asian woman from an outside country. India has a definitive caste system, and the people are openly racist towards other Asians.

This became apparent as soon as we'd arrived at the airport, when I was asked if Jum was my son's hired nanny. Although I almost laughed at the absurdity of the question, I didn't tell Jum about this conversation because, well, she would have been very upset indeed.

Then I started to think about my son. Tom was going to have to adjust to a whole new way of life here in India. I realised that I hadn't really spent too much time talking with him during the last few weeks. I should have at least encouraged him to learn a little more about the schools and the education system. But who was I trying to kid? There was always an excuse to do something else, so I had just about managed to check out three Bangalore school websites, and spent less than five minutes on each one.

I'd faced similar challenges myself all those years ago, but I'd had my brother and sister to back me up. Tom was alone when it came to sibling rivalry, or support.

This wasn't just about me; that much I knew.

As I climbed into the warm bath I decided to do what I did best. I would draw up a plan – of sorts. This plan would actually *mean* something, with timelines, objectives and all kinds of goals. No more debts to fret about, no more night-shifts – in fact, it would be bloody amazing.

After my bath I got dressed in shorts and one of the new shirts that Jum had bought for me back in Glasgow. The sleeping beauties were still smashing zeds out of the park, so I grabbed my wallet and left the room, closing the door

Good Morning India

softly behind me.

The plan could wait. I decided to get some local currency out of the nearest ATM machine and go for a little stroll. The Sonata offices were only half a mile away, and I may as well get myself orientated.

There was a bank just a few hundred yards away, and I checked out the ATM machine in the lobby before producing my card. The cash machine had the familiar VISA symbol, and I'd used the same one during my last trip to Bangalore. As I punched in my PIN number I noticed that the traffic was as busy as ever, and the smell of exhaust fumes seemed almost overwhelming.

The card was returned a little quicker than normal and the words 'Please refer to your bank' flashed up on the screen.

Great! If this wasn't a bad omen, I didn't know what was!

I decided to try Jum's card, and swore inwardly as the same message taunted me once more. What an absolutely awesome start! Here I was in my chosen new home and I couldn't even extract a single Rupee from the sodding cash machine.

I walked back towards the hotel, and the spring had most definitely gone from my step. I took the stairs instead of the lift, and by the time I reached our room I was fairly drained. Jum and Tom were awake and I needed a shower – it really was already that hot outside. Tom was engrossed in the Alienware Laptop we'd bought just before leaving Mum and Dad. This was to be a familiar sight that I'd soon get used to. The machine had cost an arm and a leg, a top-of-the-range gaming laptop that he had talked about for months. After the less than enjoyable few months that we'd had, we decided to buy him something that he'd wanted for so long.

'Where you been love?' Jum asked anxiously.

She rolled her eyes as I explained the card debacle. We'd have to call our bank and get the buggers unblocked. This was easy enough, because I still had my PepsiCo Blackberry with international roaming enabled.

After a few minutes my card had been unblocked and I explained to the operator that my wife's card was in a similar state, and passed the phone to Jum. But whilst my own conversation had gone extremely smoothly, my wife hit

Bangkok to Ben Nevis Backwards!

an issue right from the start.

She was repeating her date of birth, and the operator didn't seem impressed. Eventually she passed the phone back to me and I was surprised to learn that NatWest bank had a different date of birth on their records.

We'd spent two hours in their Glasgow bank a few days earlier to ensure this kind of cock-up didn't happen, but the service operator explained that there was no way Jum's card could be unblocked until we returned to the UK.

This was a problem. A massive problem. Most of our equity from the house sale had been moved to Jum's bank account, and this card was the only access we had to those funds.

Then I remembered that I was fully set up on the Internet banking portal. I powered up the PepsiCo laptop and, after negotiating my way onto the Presidential Hotel's Wi-Fi, I logged into my online banking account. I checked all of the details and was pleased to see a rather more healthy balance than the one I had become used to. I then logged into Jum's online account, or at least I tried to.

My plan was simple. I would transfer her balance over to mine and that would be that. Except I failed at the first hurdle, because the system would not give me visibility of her account – probably down to the card still being blocked. Mine were now visible thanks to the phone call I'd made.

I was determined not to get annoyed – after all, I still had a fair wedge in my account and I was still being paid by PepsiCo with a job offer *almost* on the table.

Ah. About that job offer...

From the outset I had been advised by my Indian soon-to-be-superiors to follow a certain route, something that I had clearly disregarded. But for the record, here it is:

1. Sell the house
2. Leave Tom and Jum in UK and go to India
3. Thrash out job offer
4. Find house
5. Find school
6. Return for Tom and Jum... and Megan
7. Start new life in India...

I was never that good at following plans, despite my talent at devising them. I knew that if I came to India alone,

Good Morning India

I would worry about Jum and Tom staying with Mum and Dad. I'd not be able to concentrate on the job in hand, quite literally. So, I'd arrived mob-handed; only poor Megan was kept on standby.

The problem with this approach was that we'd have to return to the UK in order to get the correct visas. I couldn't even apply for these until I had a firm job offer. Tom couldn't start school until he had the correct stamps in his British Passport either. This would cost a serious amount of cash, that much was certain.

Not for the first time, my lack of forethought was threatening to knock over the very first hurdle.

But I did have an idea that would soon come to life, and the outcome would influence our immediate future, but more of that later. For now, I'd have to get the best job offer I could and we'd have to find some decent accommodation, plus a good school for Tom. This didn't worry me, but I knew Jum had serious reservations about two of these objectives.

As Jum drew a warm bath, Tom and I strolled to the ATM, and this time my withdrawal was successful.

I was counting the 20,000 Indian Rupees as we walked back and I could tell that Tom was noticing the vast differences all around us. Although Bangalore is a huge and vibrant city, there are plenty of cultural giveaways that serve to remind you where you are. Lazy-looking cows wandered across busy highways, with every single car avoiding these beasts thanks to their elevated status. On each corner there seemed to be a coconut seller, offering both flesh and milk for a handful of rupees. The heady stench of traffic fumes seemed to mix with the spicy aroma of street food that was being hawked by Indians of all ages.

Tom and I raised a few eyebrows, but only until we walked past each stall. The sellers soon forgot the bald man and his handsome son as they continued yelling out the name of their oh-so-special wares.

'Dad, those milkshakes look lush, can we have some?'

He was pointing at a makeshift stall selling what was known locally as Lassi. These delicious milk-and-yoghurt-based drinks tasted even better than they looked and were as cheap as anything.

'Dad, these are even better than McDonald's!'

I laughed out loud, and at that moment I thanked God

we were in India.

'Dad, I think I'll like it here, even if Mum hates it.'

I was happy that Tom felt this way because I knew he had inherited that adventurer's spirit from me. But this was the first time he'd spilt the beans regarding Jum's feelings about India. Up until now I had underestimated my son's perceptiveness, but now I realised that he was on the ball, very much so.

'Let's go to the Hard Rock for dinner,' I suggested, and this was warmly received by Tom as we both stumbled over the less-than-perfect pavement outside the hotel.

We were saluted by the bell boy, who looked more like a bell Colonel, and headed up to our room.

Jum was awake and seemed happy enough, despite the ATM debacle.

'Let's go out for dinner and check out our new city!' I hoped that after we'd eaten and had a few drinks, plus a little exploring, we could relax and at last begin enjoying all that Bangalore had to offer. My last visit had been fantastic, and although PepsiCo had paid for a more opulent hotel with all the trimmings, I didn't see why things couldn't be just as good this time around.

The receptionist looked somewhat alarmed when I told her that we planned to walk to the Hard Rock Café, and she quickly arranged for a driver to ferry us there. Instantly, Jum curled back into her glumness. As we drove through the lively part of Bangalore I tried to pique her interest, to no avail. She seemed to have relapsed into a trance, and even the bright lights of the Hard Rock Café failed to raise a smile.

Tom however was drinking in the new sights, and at least I felt I had an ally, instead of my usual position of being cornered by the two of them.

The Hard Rock Café probably wasn't the most authentic place to have our very first taste of India, apart from the Lassi, but I had promised Tom that we'd come here ever since I returned from my business trip. I told the driver not to wait because, despite the receptionist's advice, I wanted to at least walk part of the way back to the hotel, and I knew Jum needed some fresh air, too.

The Hard Rock Café was fantastic, walls chock-full of 'genuine' musical memorabilia and steaks to die for. I was a little shocked when the bill arrived, but laughed it off – after all, we'd probably not be dining here that often.

We walked through the shopping district, and it was here that Jum became very uncomfortable with the beggars. I told them both not to make eye contact, but Tom was fascinated by these wretched people and reached into his pocket for some change.

We were immediately targeted, and although they were not exactly on par with the individual intimidating beggars back home, these were en masse, and quickly became a real nuisance.

'Why are we walking?' Jum demanded to know, and I started to feel the same way. Luckily we soon flagged down a cab, and ten minutes later all three of us were back in the room, flat out.

It must have been an hour later when I was rudely awoken by a knock at the door.

'Phil... bro... are you there?'

I recognised the voice immediately and threw on a T-shirt as I padded across the floor to let in Mech. He was one of the guys I had trained on my last visit, and a real character. He was about twenty-five and had worked for Sonata for a few years. Less serious than his colleagues, we'd shared a few pints or more. I had told him where we were planning to stay, and thought nothing more of it, but he had rocked up to our room and although it was near midnight, I was happy to see his beaming face.

I was even more pleased to see that he'd brought some Indian rum along to mark the occasion.

But while the Indian rum was okay, I decided to break out the heavy guns and opened my duty free bag to produce a litre bottle of cask-strength Macallan malt whisky. This bad boy weighed in at almost 70% proof and was twice as potent as its Indian counterpart.

We sat around the corner from the two beds and were soon chatting away like long lost brothers.

At this point there was a very quiet knock at the door and Mech told me that he'd taken the liberty of ordering some snacks. Before I could move he had sprung to his feet and pulled the door open to reveal a room service chap who couldn't have been more than four foot tall.

Mech was about my height, and he seemed delighted to find a fellow Bangalorean who was smaller than himself. But a moment later his face changed.

'Sir, what is this?' Mech demanded, pointing to a rather stingy pile of crisps on a saucer.

'Sir, these are the snacks that you kindly ordered earlier.'

Mech picked the crisps up, ate a few, and returned the remainder to the tiny plate.

'Sir, do you know who this man is?'

The room service guy shot me a concerned look, and his lack of recognition needed no verbal reply.

'This is Mister Hall, of PepsiCo... Mister *Hall* of Walkers... Walkers Crisps!'

He announced my name as if I were Gary Lineker himself, and I was beginning to worry that this tirade would wake up Jum; it was pretty late by now, and although she was a heavy sleeper, if woken all three of us would be in deep water.

'These crisps are embarrassing, please remove them from this room and come back with Walker's crisps... nothing less!'

The poor chap disappeared and I poured a large measure of Macallan into Mech's empty glass. He'd not noticed that I'd replaced his measly rum with four fingers of Scotland's finest. I raised my own glass and we both knocked the entire contents down in one.

By God it was a lovely drink, but way stronger than normal Macallan ! I coughed a little as the golden dynamite slid down my throat. When I opened my eyes and looked in Mech's direction, he had disappeared. I looked down; Mech was writhing on the floor and looked to be in a bad way.

'Phil, what the hell is this stuff?'

Despite the fine pedigree of the beverage and the fact that Mech had asked for some 'real' Scotch whisky when I'd told him I was coming back, this clearly hadn't hit the spot.

The door opened slowly and our crisp messenger reappeared with a large bowl of potato snacks. (They weren't Walkers. but that was fine as I wasn't really a huge fan.) He seemed rather pleased with himself, and even more jubilant when he spotted his nemesis twitching on the carpet.

I thanked him and helped poor Mech back onto his chair.

'Phil, I have to go, bro,' he murmured.

With that he disappeared just as quickly as he had arrived, and I decided to call it a night.

ME AND THE BOYS FROM SONATA

Breakfast in the President was a fairly grand affair, with a large buffet surrounding the inner walls of the room and at least a dozen waiting staff. They all seemed delighted when Tom appeared; even the waiters were asking if they could take selfies with my son. He loved the attention, and while this was going on I asked Jum how she was.

'I'm okay,' she murmured.

I knew this meant otherwise but was afraid to delve any deeper. I was going in to the Sonata offices today and had already formulated my plan; it went a little like this:

1. Meet everyone, especially the Boss man
2. Listen to the Offer
3. Speak with Jum
4. Look at Schools
5. Look at Houses
6. Make Counter Offer
7. Decide on House
8. Decide on School

Bangkok to Ben Nevis Backwards!

9. Return for Visas
10. Return with Visas
11. Move into House
12. Tom starts School
13. I start Job
14. Megan joins us

Not much to do, then!

Each day that we remained in the Presidential was costing about £75 – and that didn't include extra spending. When I'd let Anil from Sonata know that I was selling my house, he assumed that I'd pocket at least £200,000 from the proceeds. I wish that were the case, but only a fraction of that amount was actually received from the sale, and most of that was in an account that we couldn't even touch for now.

Jum and Tom seemed happy to stay at the hotel while I made my way in to the Offices. It took far longer than I had expected, and by the time I saw the familiar Sonata logo I was hot and bothered.

After I'd been waiting a few minutes in the reception Anil appeared behind the doors of the tiny lift, and his beaming smile was a welcome sight.

'Hey Phil, so you are here then!'

Yes I was, and I was in the mood to get straight down to business – or at least, that was the plan.

We convened in one of the more salubrious conference rooms, and I was aware that three of the more senior Sonata staff were waiting for me. The table had jugs of fresh tea and some biscuits had been laid out. (I wasn't sure if this was for my benefit or if it was their usual hangout.)

They all stood up and we shook hands. Mr Murtthy, the vice-president, smiled and asked me to sit.

'So Phil, let's discuss the offer.'

He was holding up an envelope with my name on it. It appeared that a deal had already been struck, with or without my input. I supposed this saved time.

He slid the envelope across the table and as I looked at the name on the paper, I felt as if I was in some surreal game of poker. I loved a little gamble, but this time the stakes were higher than my usual blinds. Before coming over this time, I had done a little reading up on the Indian

Good Morning India

culture, specifically business culture. These guys loved to barter, but this definitely wasn't one of my strong points.

I pulled the offer letter out of the envelope, and before I looked at the bottom line I thought about what I'd like to see.

I'd anticipated the following outgoings, based on what I'd found on Google and from chats with my buddies in the offshore IT team:

- Monthly rent – 20,000 INR
- Monthly food – 10,000 INR
- Monthly entertainment – 20,000 INR
- Monthly travel – 10,000 INR
- School Fees – 20,000 INR

This added up to a round figure of 80,000 INR, in UK money about £800 at that particular time.

I was under no illusion that my UK salary would be met by Sonata, but I wanted to be sure I was paid reasonably nonetheless. These figures were nothing if not approximate, and in my mind I believed a local monthly salary of 140,000 INR after tax would be just fine. That would allow for an additional 60,000 INR to save each month. Indian tax is around 20%, so by my calculations, an annual salary of 1,680,000 INR was what I needed to see on the paper currently in my hand.

In my heart, I had hoped for even higher, maybe 2,000,000?

Before I looked at the figure, I smiled at my hosts and noticed they all had a similar look – a slightly inquisitive one, as if they were thinking, 'Just bloody get on with it!'

1,200,000 INR.

Surely there was some mistake?

No. The only mistake in that room was me. How foolish I had been, expecting these shrewd businessmen to offer me nearly double what I had expected! They'd clearly put some thought into this opening gambit.

If I could walk a few steps in their shoes, this is what I would be looking at right now:

A forty-something Brit who had shipped his entire family over to Bangalore without even a job offer; and who had just sold his house, so was probably minted.

Bangkok to Ben Nevis Backwards!

Wrong on the second count – but they weren't to know, and at that moment I felt like a charlatan amongst these gents, they had been playing hardball for decades and I was, for the moment, caught in their headlights.

'What do you think?' they asked.

Did they really want to hear my immediate thoughts?

'I'll need to discuss this with my family and come back to you.'

'You should drink some tea and let us explain the role that we'd like you to do, please.'

I agreed, then spent an hour or more listening to the job description that they had clearly put a lot of thought into. Apparently I was to be 'Brand Champion' for PepsiCo, a grand title with some pretty intense remits on my part. Not only would I head up the offshore service desk, I'd also be responsible for setting up two new ones for their USA based customers – and I'd be expected to take part in regular travel back to the UK and to Australia.

I could get used to that part of the job, but not on that salary. I needed to know what these guys were on so at least I would have an idea of what I should be aspiring to.

I was about to mention my desired amount when Anil asked me to pop out for a minute.

'Phil, I have something for you in my office,' he said politely.

I had no idea what to expect, but as we entered his small work space and he slid the door shut my heart sank as I recognised the somewhat mashed-up box on his table.

Three weeks earlier Jum had insisted that we buy a hundred tins of Cesar dogfood. This was obviously for Megan, but I did have reservations. They fell on deaf ears, so I decided just to go with the flow. We bought the dog food and, after boxing it up, went to the Spean Bridge Post Office to send it off to Bangalore. The whole operation cost over £400, and I had had many misgivings about the fate of these canine comestibles.

Fast forward three weeks or so and here I was, reunited with the very same box of tricks – but clearly the tins had suffered severely in transit. The Sonata flies were having a field day and poor Anil's diminutive office stank to high heaven.

I wondered what was going through his mind. He had surely shared this hilarious arrival with Murtthy and co…

Good Morning India

How could I expect to barter with these fellows if they already knew what a dipstick they were dealing with?

'I'll drive you to the hotel with the box, we'll leave now.'

He had no argument from me, and after being dropped off at the President with my stinking cargo, I was pretty much done for the day.

To his credit, Anil was a true gentleman. He probably dined out on this little faux pas for months – possibly still is today – but he was a real professional, and for that I'll always respect him.

The real sting in the tail was the fact that after we disposed of the rotten Cesar cargo, I noticed that Bangalore pet shops sold the same brand for considerably less than back in the UK!

Once back in the room, after having explained the whole dog food debacle to Jum, I noticed my Blackberry was having a fit. Richard's name appeared on the screen. He was one of the reasons my life had become so miserable over the last 12 months, and I just could not be bothered to speak to the opinionated buffoon right now. I switched off the phone.

Chapter 5

Plan B

I'd been told by Murtthy and the boys that I had around a week or so to either agree with their terms or come back with a counter offer. My PepsiCo contract would end on the last day in October, and if I hadn't made up my mind by then, either way I would be a free agent.

I left for work quite early the next day, with Jum and Tom still snoozing deep in the Presidential Hotel. For some reason I could think more easily when walking, and by the time I'd reached the Sonata office block I had come up with a few ideas.

Anil called me into his office before I'd reached my own part of the building. He had an earnest look on his face as we sat down.

'Phil, what is your Plan B? You must have at least one extra plan when you are in this type of situation.'

Anil then explained that in his culture, all businessmen would have a backup plan just in case their preferred one didn't make the grade. He seemed to sense that I was far from focussed, and he questioned my thought process as far as bringing my wife and son was concerned.

'You should have come alone, accept offer, find school, find house and then go back for family,' he said gently.

I couldn't even try to explain; clearly we came from two different worlds. This man had worked very hard to get where he was today, and now he was a middle manager in a large Indian firm, with a wife who was a dentist, two children, a car, and a house of their own. I knew that Anil had long planned for this, and was still planning for so much more, whereas I had stumbled through life, by some luck making it to forty-five with a small family, and was still clumsily playing Blackjack with the cards of life as they were dealt.

Perhaps it was time to put an end to this approach?

I thanked Anil for his considerate words and spent the rest of the day listening to helpdesk calls from my new team.

By the end of the day I had it figured out. My new To Do list went something like this:

1. Find School for Tom
2. Find House for all of us
3. Renegotiate Offer
4. If Counter Offer is not accepted, revert to Plan B
5. What is Plan B?

Yep, pretty accurate – I really hadn't thought about a backup plan; perhaps, deep down, fear of failing was the real root of my evil.

The next two weeks were a right old mixture of Indian chaos, British stubbornness, and a fair dash of culture-related learning curves. We'd found a decent school for Tom without too much hassle; they even followed the UK education system, and he was looking forward to the whole affair. The problem was that until we all had the right visas, he couldn't start the next leg of his education – but even before that, we needed a house.

I had no idea that it would be so bloody difficult to find rented accommodation in India!

Bangalore is a huge city with major traffic issues, and we needed a place that was no further than three or four miles from the Sonata offices. Anil did his level best to accompany us on our searches, but sometimes he was simply too busy.

After several aborted attempts to find somewhere suitable we were shown a serviced apartment in the Jaynagar part of Bangalore. It looked great. The two-bedroomed spacious flat was unfurnished, but had air conditioning and good security. It also had access to a large swimming pool. It seemed ideal.

Owning a dog had been a major problem so far when house hunting, but in this case the agent had indicated

Plan B

that this was 'no issue'. We agreed to meet the owner a few days later but when we arrived – three of us plus Anil – there clearly was 'an issue'.

After about twenty minutes of raised voices and with more than a few dirty looks in my direction, Anil shook his head and told me, 'He doesn't want to give.'

But it seemed that Megan was not the problem. The agent hadn't told the owner that we were Europeans, and this had thrown a spanner in the rental works.

At first I thought the bloke was being racist, but I soon realised that he was after a quick deal and didn't want to register the rental details with the Tax authorities. Any non-Indian living and working in the country would need to inform the authorities, and this would take a fat slice of the landlord's profits – so we were back to square one: homeless.

In between these minor disasters, the Hall family were getting to know a little more about India and her ways. This country was nowhere near as free-thinking as I had originally imagined; there was even more red tape to deal with here than back home. Perhaps this was one of the legacies left behind by my own countrymen from the days of the Raj?

Bloody permits! You needed one for almost everything, and a few more besides.

Plan B was starting to look more appealing, although I had yet to mention this to my wife and child – the idea was still germinating.

On the way back to the hotel, which was costing me a small fortune by now, Anil had one more ace up his sleeve. 'Phil, there is a house for rent that we should look at, not far from here.'

It was almost 10 p.m. and although I had felt like we were done for the day, I begrudgingly agreed to check it out. As we pulled over in the leafy, wide side road, I could see the houses here were both large and attractive, and within minutes of setting foot in this new place, Jum seemed as happy as I had seen her in recent times. Tom was keen as well, so I told Anil as much.

The monthly rent was about 20,000 INR – £200 in UK money.

Bangkok to Ben Nevis Backwards!

Although the garden was tiny, there was a large roof area we could use – a common theme in Indian houses.

The place was owned by a Judge, no less, and Anil promised to take me to meet him the next morning.

Dear Mr Murtthy,

I thank you for your kind offer. After careful consideration, I have decided to lodge a counter offer with yourselves.

Taking into careful consideration the role that I have been offered, and also the fact that I will be required to fly my family back to the UK and obtain three visas, I hereby suggest the following terms and conditions:

- *A salary of no less than 2 million INR annually;*

- *A cash payment/bonus of 300,000 INR at the end of my first month to cover all costs of my family's visas and flights to and from London to apply for these visas.*

I would much appreciate your response within the next twenty-four hours if possible. Many thanks.

Best Regards,
Phil Hall

That should do the trick.

Of course I would take a slight reduction on the salary, but I would not budge as far as the 300k was concerned. These guys had some rather lofty plans for me, so now I was putting their commitment to the test. They had one full day in which to reply, and after that... well, Plan B was ready and waiting!

But what a twenty-four hours!

Firstly, the Judge/landlord decided to visit me at the Sonata office, and after a good ten minutes of diatribe he came out with it:

'Because you are a wealthy businessman, I want to increase the monthly rental by one hundred percent.'

Plan B

He stared directly into my eyes, and all I could see in his was Plan B... yes, it kept on coming back to me.

I smiled at him. 'I don't think so.'

I stood up and excused myself, from my own office!

It was nearly lunchtime, and instead of joining my new work buddies I decided now was the time to reveal Plan B to Jum and Tom. I almost sprinted back to the President and was pleased to see my family just sitting down for their midday meal, so over lunch I explained why I was feeling so happy. As ever, I had written the plan down so I knew it off by heart:

1. Listen to refusal of counter offer – there was no way they'd accept
2. Book three flights to Thailand
3. Leave

Yes, it really was this simple. The best plans always are.

I was met with confused but hopeful stares. 'Phil, why you want to go Thailand?' Jum had a knack of coming straight out with it; bush beating wasn't something she had even heard of.

I explained that I'd always wanted to put my BA to use and do some teaching. Tom could go to the same school that I'd taught at, and he'd be surrounded by family – something he'd not experienced before. And Jum – well, she'd be back with her Mum. Surely these were good enough reasons?

After lunch we went up to our room and I decided to call in sick for the rest of the day. India wasn't really working out for us, and there was no way that I'd return to the UK. Our home had been sold, I had no job, and my parents were in no state to help – and why should I expect them to?

My Blackberry rang at that moment, and I was delighted to hear Mum's voice on the other end. We spoke for about five minutes; all I wanted was to ask how she and Dad were, but she seemed more interested in our news. Instead of telling her my new plans, I reassured her that we were doing well.

'Is Megan with you yet?'

Oh God! I had all but forgotten about our little ball of white fluff! After the phone call I checked my emails and realised that she was due to fly out in two days!

I hurriedly called the pet export people, and was so relieved to hear that she was fine – but even more so when they agreed to look after her for as long as it took for us to sort out our plans.

'Okay, let's go to Thailand!' Jum and Tom chorused together, and that was just what I needed to hear.

I started looking for tickets online, and by tea time I'd booked three single flights from Bangalore to Bangkok for the following evening – job done!

Sure, I still had to refuse the offer, and if I were Anil – well, I would probably be more than a little peeved. But right now I was only worried about my own little clan, and I knew he would ultimately be cool. Richard would be a different matter, but as we had plenty of cash in the bank, I wasn't overly concerned about him getting his claws into the rest of my monthly salary... and he would.

After an early dinner, we went out for a walk and I did my best to reassure them that India had been just a blip; our real future was just a three-hour flight away.

I slept rather well that night, and in the morning we packed again and I kissed Jum goodbye before setting off for the Sonata offices, for the last time. I had a few more things on my list:

- Change the gazillion INR that I'd been withdrawing every day before we left for the house deposit; INR cannot be used outside India
- Chase the air tickets up if they hadn't arrived by lunchtime

Everything else could wait until we were in Thailand. I could use a holiday after the last three weeks of chasing around after houses and suchlike, and no doubt Jum and Tom would feel the same way.

On arriving I was surprised to see Anil and the Judge having a conversation in the reception area. What could they be talking about?

'Phil, Mr Singh is here to discuss your rental, he wants you to take the house at the original price!'

Plan B

Great, I had to come up with something quick because I didn't want to disappoint Anil – the Judge, I could care less about.

'Anil, I need to speak with you. Mr Singh, please leave your number and I will call you later.' I surprised myself with the way these words rolled out, effortless and without any hesitation.

Anil responded: 'Phil, Murtthy is waiting for you – please come to the main meeting room.'

Hmmm, this would be the showdown that I was dreading. In my mind I had played this neatly out, and it was all going wrong. I'd have preferred to have a little word with Anil first and then make my excuses and leave, but no, that wasn't going to happen.

As we entered the meeting room, I was surprised to see no less than five of Murtthy's associates waiting for myself and Anil. I was introduced to each of them, and noticed a familiar-looking offer letter directly in front of my chair.

'Please Philip; open the letter so that we may welcome you to Sonata!' Murtthy sounded almost excited, and as I sat down and opened up the envelope, I start to feel a little light headed.

Things were not going to plan, not at all.

But I had to stick to my guns, and before I removed the contents of the envelope I addressed the room in my best business voice – whatever that means.

'It was very nice to meet you all, but I have some bad news.'

Their faces looked concerned, and I felt somewhat guilty.

'As you may or may not know, my wife is Thai and yesterday we had some bad news, her mother is not well.'

Although this wasn't exactly the truth, it was close enough.

'I have decided that we should go to her hometown immediately and take care of her mother.'

'Family is important,' Murtthy declared, and the whole table nodded in unison.

And that was that. They were very gracious, and even agreed to keep my offer open for six months – total gents to a fault!

The rest of the day was a blur; Anil helped me to change the INR to dollars and even called up the airlines to expe-

Bangkok to Ben Nevis Backwards!

dite our tickets. I couldn't have imagined my PepsiCo boss, Richard Jones, would have lifted a single finger to help.

Speaking of which, the news must have travelled fast because as I handed my company laptop and Blackberry back, I could see his name flashing on the screen.

Anil also noticed. 'Would you like to speak with Richard?'

I shook my head and he gave me an understanding smile as we shook hands for the last time ever.

I'd just like to say that Anil was the most professional and helpful manager I'd ever met, and it would have been a pleasure to work with him under different circumstances.

Less than ten hours later we were on the plane *en route* to Bangkok. It was as if Bangalore had merely been a lengthy stop over – and a very expensive one at that.

Jum and Tom were soon catching up with their sleep and as I reached into my jacket pocket, I realised that the Sonata offer letter was inside.

'What the hell...' I said to myself, and decided to read it, regardless.

What I found shook me.

They'd agreed to the new salary, and in addition the 300k one-off payment had been sanctioned!

I smiled to myself, feeling a great deal of self-worth mixed with a large dose of confusion. Had I made the right choice? Well, at least this offer had a six month expiry date, and who knows if I would be back one day?

I closed my eyes and, in what seemed like minutes later, opened them to see a bright Thai sun beaming through the window.

We had arrived in the Land of Smiles!

Chapter 5

THE LAND OF SMILES

Every time – and there had been many – that I came to Thailand, I always felt the same: happy. Very happy! I couldn't quite put my finger on why this was, I just knew that this was the place where I always had a really good time, and I was determined to make this Plan B work. Although it wasn't our last chance, I started to get my mindset ready for what would be probably the biggest challenge of our lives so far.

By comparison, India had been pretty much laid out for us – well at least my job was ready and waiting, but issues started to arise as we dug a little deeper. So how would Thailand compare?

Well, it was Jum's home country and I could already sense her happiness as she chatted in Thai to a lady in the seats behind us. They were talking about what every Thai seemed to love discussing: food! It's no secret that Thai food is amongst the most popular in the world, and with good reason. Indian food was great, but the lack of pork and beef meant that my wife never really took to that particular cuisine. And as we walked through the customs area and into the arrivals section of Suvarnabhumi Airport, I could already detect the distinct aroma of Thai food.

I'd originally started travelling to Thailand back in the 1980s; it was very different all those years ago, but now even the airport had been upgraded. This was far more modern than the rather ramshackle Don Muang facility that had been replaced some five years earlier, in 2006. I kind of missed the old place, but here we were in 2011 –

and this time it wasn't a holiday. We had come to Thailand to start a new life.

Hang on; weren't those the same sentiments I'd had when we'd turned up into Bangalore almost four weeks earlier? We'd spent almost £2,000 during that fruitless month, and although the cost of living in Thailand wasn't expensive, finding somewhere to live, transport, and all the other trimmings would soon stack up.

Plus, I was currently unemployed.

Tom had been out of the education system since the beginning of the UK summer holidays. I wasn't on course to win the Father of the Year Award, so I'd already constructed a new list – hopefully a little more successful than its predecessors:

1. Go to Kalasin, probably check into Rimpao Hotel
2. Relax for a few days
3. Contact Jum's family
4. Sort out her bank card – if I could... my funds were running low
5. Look for somewhere to live
6. Find a good school for Tom
7. Find a job for me
8. Finally, bring Megan over
9. Start living life

Okay, the last point was a given, but to be honest our lives had been in limbo ever since we'd left Wallingford, and I felt wholly responsible.

Visa-wise, we'd entered on our UK passports and had a 30-day stamp. We'd need to look into a tourist visa for 60 days thereafter and hopefully I'd be working soon so I could make arrangements for a work permit and a non-Immigration visa that would cover the whole family. Jum's Thai passport had long since expired and was back in the UK with Mum and Dad. She was travelling on her British documents.

We soon found a restaurant in the public part of the airport, and after ordering her favourite dishes my wife started to unwind.

The difference between this airport and the one that we'd just left were an indication of how different India and

The Land of Smiles

Thailand are, despite their relatively close proximity. Indian people are very polite on the whole, and I really liked them, but Thai people have a totally different aura. Even the airport officials had a ready smile for us, and I soon noticed how attractive the Thai woman were – sorry if that sounds rather sexist, but it was one of the reasons why I felt so happy over here! Back in the UK, the fair sex had evolved to a point where I found them rather over-competitive and almost androgynistic.

Men and woman are equal, and I understood that the old-fashioned gender terminology had all but disappeared, but I felt things had been taken too far. Only a year earlier I had been lambasted by a colleague at PepsiCo for referring to a customer as a 'manageress':

'She is a manager who happens to be a lady!'

Well, that told me.

In Thailand, they have a polite particle that is definitely gender related. Men will end a sentence with the word 'Krup'. Ladies will use 'Ka'.

I'll not dwell on the differences between the three cultures, but having spent a lot of time in at least two of these I knew where I felt more comfortable – and it wasn't back in the UK.

As the dishes arrived, I smiled inwardly as I saw how excited Jum was to revisit some of her edible memories of Thailand. Green chicken curry with egg fried rice was ordered for Tom and I, with a large helping of Pad Thai to share. These are widely known as famous Thai dishes, but are not exactly authentic. For Jum there was Somtam, a fiery papaya salad; Kor Moo Yang, a pork stew; and Nua namman Hoi, beef in oyster sauce.

We feasted on this gorgeous food and I drank a couple of Thai beers as we chatted happily about what the heck we'd do next. When I mentioned Megan, Jum couldn't hide her concern and I promised that we'd find somewhere soon and send for our beautiful substitute daughter.

I left the table to book some domestic flights to Kohn Kaen, the nearest airport to Kalasin, Jum's home city.

We had decided to follow my carefully written plan, and less than four hours later we were all chilling out around the Rimpao Hotel's large swimming pool, where we continued to enjoy some of the best food that Thailand had to offer. After a short walking tour of the city, we retired to our room and, as Tom got stuck into his gaming laptop and reconnected with friends back in the old country, Jum shared her immediate concerns with me.

She was worried about the Thai education system; how would Tom manage in a school that only spoke Thai? I pointed out that quite a few of the high schools in Kalasin had a Mini English Program (MEP), and these had at least five or six subjects that were taught in English. Of course there were also international schools, but these were hellishly expensive and had to be discounted, at least for now.

Jum was also worried about my ability to get a teaching job – and finally, she was worried about her own family. The Naenudon's were by any standards, a weird bunch. Jum had three sisters and they were all utter bitches. That isn't just my opinion, but fact.

I explained that we'd connect with her Mum but we could stay away from Bitches Number 1 and 2. As for Bitch Number 3 – well, we didn't have to bother with her because she was living in Basingstoke with my one-time best buddy. We'd naïvely acted as matchmakers some twelve years previously, and not long after Bitch Number 3 arrived, she turned my hapless buddy against me and we ceased any sort of contact thereafter.

As far as housing options were concerned, we had bought some land from Jum's 'aunty' and we could look into either selling it or perhaps building a home there. The land was in Ban Mai Chai Mongkol, the village where Jum was born.

Jum's father had died a few years earlier; in my opinion, he was the only other good member of that family. In fact we'd taken his name, Samran, as one of Tom's middle names; the other was Colin, my Dad's name.

Jum also had another concern: in Thailand everyone has to be registered to a house. This was useful for a variety of purposes, including census-related reports, and for working requirements. Without this registration, a Thai national would have problems finding a job, voting, and a myriad of other human rights-related processes.

Jum strongly believed that for whatever reasons, one of the sisters had paid a sum of money to have Jum's name struck off from the registry of the family home in Ban Mai. If true, this would be a big problem, but we'd look into this

The Land of Smiles

in a few days. Hopefully it was just an ugly rumour.

'I go to bed,' Jum announced after our discussion, and although I was fairly shattered, my mind was working overtime. Despite my latest written plan, I couldn't help but wonder exactly what would become of us.

I also spent a few minutes thinking about my parents. I couldn't really see my Dad being the Colin Hall we'd known and loved, ever again. I had read up on Vascular Dementia and there was simply no good news at all. The condition was totally irreversible, and it really did strip the afflicted of all dignity as it continued to destroy the brain cells and ravage the physical capability. Dad was 78 years old, and had been in very good health before this bastard disease knocked him flat. He would walk at least two or three miles each day and spent most of the daytime in his beloved garden.

Doctors believed that Dad had displayed the early symptoms of Dementia some time ago, although this had not been diagnosed at the time, and I was starting to realise that they were correct. Of course we'd had clashes ever since I was old enough to buy a pint of beer; it wasn't unusual for father and son to argue, especially when they shared the same home. But in recent times, these arguments were both tiresome and pretty damn annoying. Perhaps the poor man had been suffering in silence for all those years and I'd just put it all down to him being an old curmudgeon with a penchant for a verbal tear up.

I took these thoughts with me to bed, and as Jum and Tom's snores resembled a bizarre musical based on Babe, I lost consciousness – and probably drowned them out with my own contributions.

THE HALLS AND THE NAENUDONS

Chapter 7

THE BOY, THE GIRL, THE FISH AND THE SPIDER...

I had had doubts about the move to Asia, but my son Thomas was never a part of them. Perhaps it was because I didn't really think hard enough about how removing him from the relative safety and conformism of the British education system would affect his own future. Or maybe I *had* actually considered this, and selfishly put my own dreams ahead of his schooling?

But I prefer to believe that it was the fact that my son was an incredibly well developed young man who already had a better grasp on life than many people twice his age. He also shared my love of animals, knowledge and travel, and I was sure that if anything, this journey would be the making of him.

Another part of the trip that I was looking forward to was meeting up with our Thai family, despite the Three Ugly Sisters; family is family, after all, no matter what, and in my experience the kids are usually not as bad as the parents. For one reason or another, Tom had no cousins in the UK and he often brought this topic up with us. So when we decided to spend several months in the village of Jum's birth, Ban Mai Chai Mongkol, I knew that he would finally be able to connect with his extended family. What could be better than seeing my own flesh and blood having fun with his mother's relatives in the tropical sun that we had all missed for so long?

Of course, the more that you play these scenarios in your head, the higher becomes the chance of everything turning into a huge anti-climax, and after the rather disinterested

Bangkok to Ben Nevis Backwards!

reaction our arrival mustered from Jum's mother, we were only too happy to accept an invitation from her aunty, Yai Dee. In hindsight we should never have even have set foot in that village, but isn't life all about learning from your mistakes?

After a few days kicking back at Yai Dee's a few of Tom's cousins started to call around, mainly out of curiosity but also because they knew that Jum was a very generous aunty.

Pang and Spark were aged 10 and 4 respectively and were a lot of fun with no little measure of mischief mixed into the equation. Spark had the ability to maintain a runny nose 24/7. He also had a tendency to eat everything in sight, and had absolutely no issues with picking up titbits from the floor – not a good idea at Yai Dee's. His older sister, Pang, was a little more reserved at first, and seemed rather infatuated with her older cousin.

Tom adored them, and for at least a week or so there were no problems whatsoever, but isn't that always the way with kids? They would spend hours in the overgrown garden, despite Jum's constant warning of snakes – in fact that made them even more eager to set up a little camp near the large mango tree behind the diminutive house.

Tom's love of animals came directly from Jum and I, because between us we would never harm a fly unless it was unavoidable, and even then we would do our best to think of an alternative. I've even seen my wife pick up a snail or a slug on a British public footpath to avoid the inevitable careless foot that comes crashing down on just such poor unsuspecting invertebrates.

Of course, I took the animal thing a little further. We had our lovely Megan, still to join us on the adventure, but I also had my tarantulas!

Tom must have been about five or six when he first really took an interest in my fabulous furry freak show, but he soon made up for lost time. He'd even remind me when we had to feed the little monsters, and would always give a squeak of delight when he had the chance to handle the more docile gang members.

One morning he woke me up shouting, 'Daddy, the spiders are dancing!'

I had put a male and female Goliath Bird Eater Spider

together the night before in the hope that they would mate and produce hundreds of spiderlings. When I got down the stairs I realised that the 'dancing' was in fact the pair of them 'getting it on'!

We watched for about ten minutes and his little face was almost glued to the glass as the two mini titans did their thing. Eventually he had to skip off for a toilet break, which coincided nicely with the much larger female tiring of the romantic liaison; her date rapidly became her dinner.

I didn't have the heart to tell Tom that 'Rambo' hadn't survived the meeting of minds, and to this day he believes that he was sold to another collector for more of the same.

So – back to Ban Mai Chai Mongkol and the mini jungle that had become our home...

After the hustle and bustle of Bangalore, Ban Mai Chai Mongkol was a welcome change. Jum and I were winding down and slowly planning the next stage of the Hall family's life strategies, and Tom... well, he was just being Tom.

Life in Yai Dee's house was very chilled, and despite her fierce reputation as a trouble-causing little gremlin, we got on just fine. In fact, we were serious about building a house on the land in the next plot, and this began to take shape rather nicely.

Tom and his two cousins, plus about four neighbourhood kids, had started to build a little house of their own, and one day he asked me if we could perhaps buy a few fish for their hideout. A few weeks earlier we had noticed a pet fish shop of sorts, which had an abundance of Siamese fighting fish for sale. Known locally as 'Pla Gat', these little beauties only cost about fifty pence each. They would fetch at least £25 or more back in the UK, but as they were indigenous to the region I suppose it was no surprise.

We set off that afternoon, and as Jum and Tom selected the new additions to the family I negotiated my way through the vast collection of fish tanks to the customer toilet. It was pitch black, and as I fumbled for the light switch and turned it on, I nearly jumped out of my skin – about three inches from my face sat a huge Golden Orb Weaver spider!

This gorgeous specimen was at least ten inches across and had made a massive web that stretched all the way from the doorway to the sunken toilet seat. The staff had neglected to warn me about this beast, and were probably happily anticipating my screams of terror. Thankfully I loved spiders, and within a few minutes had decided to catch this one and bring it back to Yai Dee's, to release it into our new plot of land, where it could web away like billy-o and hopefully reduce the local fly and mosquito population.

Totally harmless and very chilled, the spider was soon on my arm and almost immediately starting weaving away like a good 'un. To say the shop assistant was shocked has to rank up there with the understatements of the century, or at least of 2011! When Tom and Jum noticed my new best friend the poor fighting fish they had chosen were almost forgotten, but as we paid for the three fish I noticed an extra charge had been added to the bill. Oh my days! They wanted me to pay for the bloody spider!

Okay, it was only 100 baht, but such cheek!

Welcome to Thailand!

On return to Yai Dee's house I was thinking a little about how we would cope when we Megan finally arrived. Poor little thing, after nearly six weeks in a Fife kennels, she would have probably given up on us. She was due to land in Bangkok in about a week. Yai Dee was no dog lover and I could foresee all kinds of problems ahead, but for now we had to sort out these new smaller additions to the extended Hall family.

I had no idea just how big a problem they would cause in the next couple of days.

We soon found a suitable house for the fighting fish: a large flowerpot did the trick, and Tom introduced them to his cousins and friends. I was pleasantly surprised to find an oversized sweet jar that was perfect for the Orb Weaver, now named Godzilla (courtesy of Tom). I had always had a real fascination with spiders, snakes and lizards, probably thanks to the six years I spent in South Africa as a child. I can still remember the sheer horror on Mum's face when she opened my sock drawer one day, only to be greeted by about a dozen baby bullfrogs staring back at her expectantly!

So, back to our little menagerie:

Although Tom was older than his cousin Pang, it was

pretty clear that she was the leader of the little group and, due to his good nature, he was happy enough to let her rule the roost. She seemed a little out of sorts when she marched into the camp to find the flowerpot filled with water and complete with mini-denizens, and she wasted no time at all in taking a much closer look.

Since arriving at Yai Dee's I had found an excellent place to do my job searching online, and the mini-veranda allowed me almost perfect visual access to most of the front garden and the little road beyond. I had got to know my Thai niece and nephew rather well during the few weeks we had been in Ban Mai, and Pang was one of those kids who was always very loud unless she was up to no good.

About a day after the fish had been installed, Tom and Jum had borrowed Yai Dee's moped and were out for the afternoon looking at local schools (more of that later). Goon, one of Jum's sisters (Bitch Number 2), had appeared at around 10 a.m., and Pang was sat in the back of the pickup truck with a few of her cronies. I had started to notice that Goon never materialised if my wife was around, and I was beginning to see a pattern that made me feel a little uneasy.

As she shuffled into the house I could hear Yai Dee complaining that Goon always seemed to leave her kids with Yai Dee at the last moment, and although my Thai wasn't great I was sure I heard Goon refer to my wife as 'Kwai'.

'Kwai' translated to 'water buffalo', and was probably the second worst personal insult you could level at an individual here in Thailand. (The lowest would be 'Ee-hia' – a water monitor.) Of course the water denominator had nothing to do with the overall sentiment, but it shocked me and was a sign of things to come.

I realised that Pang also hadn't bothered saying hello, and was just about to get back to my game of online poker – I mean, job seeking assignment – when I heard a splashing noise.

Pang was fishing around in the flower pot as the other two kids watched in total silence. She appeared to have caught one of the fish in her hand, and held the tiny thing in her fist as she counted to ten in Thai: 'nung song sarm see hah hok jet bpairt...' (1 2 3 4 5 6 7 8...)

'Pang! Stop!' I shouted at the top of my lungs, and she

dropped the barely-alive fish back into the water and gave me a look that made me feel like a water monitor's lowly servant.

'Farang Suber!' she muttered – 'Stupid Foreigner!'

Yai Dee, Yai Leew and Goon came running out and demanded to know what was going on. I walked over to the flowerpot and immediately Pang burst into crocodile tears. I checked out the floundering fish, starved of oxygen, and was relieved to see it eventually swim down to safety and away from any ten-year-old executioner's sweaty little hands.

By now Pang was in full flow; she wasted no time telling her new audience how the evil Phil had scared her for no reason whatsoever.

Now, I hate any form of animal cruelty but I did have to bite my tongue for once. Firstly I was in someone else's home, and secondly I was completely outnumbered here. There was Yai Dee, a force on her own; her girlfriend Yai Liew, who had a face that would stop an army – they both had breath that would do any water monitor, or buffalo, proud – and there was Goon.

All three were looking daggers at me, and I didn't fancy my chances one bit. But I explained the whole scenario in my sketchy Thai and was surprised, even relieved, when all three adults burst into laughter!

'It only a fish!' said Goon in pidgin English, between gulps of oxygen – and this was the first time I actually saw Yai Dee smile.

I felt both angry and confused, and as I turned to walk back to my laptop I heard another splash, followed by a tiny splat. The broken body of a beautiful Siamese Fighting Fish lay motionless just behind me, and now I heard six sets of laughter ringing in my ears.

I had to hold back the tears – it wasn't easy – and then my utter anger as I saw Goon trample what was left of the fish into mush.

Resisting the urge to do something rash, I shouted at the top of my lungs, 'Nooooooo!'

This actually had the desired effect, and within a minute the pickup had gone, complete with murderers, and Thailand's version of Thelma and Louise had returned to whatever it was they were doing previously.

I did notice a look of utter contempt from the pair of them, and briefly wondered why the hell we had even bothered coming to this blasted village in the first place!

But after a few games of computer poker I had started to chill out, and I took a little break from the virtual table to check up on Godzilla. She had webbed the sweet jar into submission and was chowing down on a large cockroach I had found in my shoe yesterday.

Yai Dee had so far ignored her new lodger, but I was wondering how long it would be before this mini marvel would end up sharing the fate of the poor fish.

A few hours later Jum and Tom pulled up on the battered moped and I could see tears welling up in my son's eyes as I described the earlier incident.

'Phil, I know you love animals but Thai people are different.' Jum explained to me how fish are simply food and nothing more to village people. I understood, but pointed out that there was no need for such cruelty, and she just smiled her winning smile.

This is why I loved her so much. Despite being brought up in a totally different world, Jum had transformed into an animal lover and one of her conditions of this transworld expedition was that under no terms would she leave our Westie behind. Megan was one of the family, probably placed a little higher than me, depending on my behaviour on any given day.

The price of bringing our Westie to Asia was well over £1000, more than all three humans put together. I started to have real doubts about how she would cope in the heat and humidity that North East Thailand was famous for, but I was even more worried about the people who shared the same oxygen as us, especially after the mini horror show I had not long witnessed. I could understand how the two cultures were so different but cruelty was something that I could never accept, and my concern for Megan was growing.

We held a mini-burial for the departed fighting fish, and this attracted the attention of the aging lovers – Yai Dee and Yai Leew. To say that they were mystified was an understatement – in fact, Yai Dee at first thought we were using the remains of the fish as a trap for rats. She loved nothing more than *noo-yang*, grilled rat, and was ready to scuttle off to make some sauces to accompany this village delicacy, until Jum explained the whole ceremony to her.

Throwing her arms up in disgust and spitting out a puddle of purple phlegm, she sloped off into the back garden muttering all kinds of Isaan derogatory terms. Yai Leew soon followed, but only after spitting her own betel nut residue all over the grave of our expired fish buddy.

I shook my head and started to think about an escape plan. Surely we couldn't stay with these people another day?!

Then Jum reminded me about our long term plans. Indeed, we had already bought the adjoining plot and were supposed to be building our new home here, next door to Yai Dee.

This reminded me of another reason that had filled my mind with doubt shortly after pitching up Ban Mai about three weeks earlier. Around four or five years earlier we had agreed that buying some land in the village was a sound investment. For the very reasonable sum of around £800 we had negotiated a deal with Yai Dee and she agreed to sell us some land – probably slightly smaller than a football pitch, with more than enough space to build a decent home with some garden to spare. We had sent the money off in two instalments, and nothing more had been said.

Until the day we arrived in Ban Mai, when we learnt exactly how different my wife was to her mother.

Yai Kit, Jum's mum, had been less than pleased to see her second eldest daughter; she could barely muster a grunt as we approached her, all *wais* and *sawadees*. She finally asked what we were doing there, as if we had no reason to come back to the place of Jum's birth and family home. Jum explained that our Indian Odyssey had not gone to plan, but here we were, back in Ban Mai – and how happy we were to see her again!

Yai Kit seemed distinctly unimpressed and told us in no uncertain terms that we couldn't stay. This came as a shock and I could hear my wife's voice wavering as she took the news on board; our suitcases were piled up outside the house like a herd of pink elephants.

According to Yai Kit, as the house now belonged to Hoi, Jum's younger sister, she had no say in whether we could stay or not. (I'll explain a little more about that particular individual a little later, a real sweetheart...not!)

After listening for several minutes to the reasons why we couldn't stay here, after five years away, Jum looked at me and told me how sorry she was. My poor dear wife felt ashamed of the fact that she was no longer welcome at her family home. Her father, Samran, had passed away two years earlier, and with his death all traces of Jum's connection with her family seemed to vanish.

About two years before Samran's passing, a seemingly insignificant event took place that somehow spiralled out of control and change my wife's relationship with her family forever. It also put paid to a very long friendship of mine.

We were visiting Shaun and Doi in nearby Basingstoke, and even though the relationship wasn't anything to write home about, we were still on speaking terms. The original plan was for us to stay for a few days, but we never made it past the first couple of hours.

My friend had change beyond recognition since marrying Jum's sister; his attitude had altered so dramatically that I guess this relationship was doomed from that day forward. I'll not bore you with the details, but suffice to say that from the moment we set foot inside their home on that Saturday morning, I had never felt less welcome in my whole life. Pretty much everything we said was met with some kind of aggressive and unfriendly response.

I suppose the breaking point came when Tom was staring out of their French door window and Shaun walked up and let out a full fart about an inch away from his head.

I remembered years earlier when the two of them had clashed over some stupid little toy and Shaun had shouted very loudly in Tom's face – he was only about four years old at the time. I also remembered a time when Shaun was chasing my son around our house in Wallingford and Tom had hidden behind the bathroom door. Shaun ran up the stairs and flung the door open, smashing Tom full in the face. He came bawling down the stairs and ran into my arms. Shaun was adamant that it wasn't on purpose, but refused to apologise.

Who the hell was this creep? I wondered now.

There were other even less savoury incidents, and all were underlined by that sour-faced bitch he was married to.

So we left their home and I sent him an email, not exactly my style, telling him in no uncertain terms what I thought of his pretty crappy behaviour over the last 10 years. There was no reply, but about a month later we received a phone call from Jum's parents.

Typically Jum would love these interactions, and her sing-song voice always made me feel warm inside. But this time she hardly spoke a word.

I could just about make out the tones of her mother and Jum's body language told me that something terrible had happened. Someone had died, perhaps?

After the call she sat back down on the sofa and said nothing.

'Jum, what's happened love?' I placed an arm around her and expected some sobbing, but there was nothing.

Those bastards had really done a number on us. In a nutshell, they had gathered up 'information' from a Thai forum that I used, and sent this in paper format to Mum and Dad Naenudon. They had also gone to the expense of having it translated into Thai.

It was bad, very bad indeed. According to the document, I had pretty much slagged off the whole family with every opportunity I could muster. I called them gold-diggers, dishonest, and basically they were the scum of the earth.

Of course, this was not the truth. I held them in high regard and would never say or write a bad word about them, especially not on a public forum which I knew Shaun has access to.

But that didn't matter. Samran and his wife believed these lies. They were heartbroken; why wouldn't they be?

They told Jum that we were never to set foot in their home again.

Despite the financial help that I had given them and the money that Jum worked hard for and sent over every month, they were saying goodbye.

I did my best to disprove these accusations – my friend who ran the forum even sent me the original archive copies in case I wanted to open up a lawsuit, bless him. But these were simple folk and they chose to believe a pair of lying scum bags.

For that, I will never ever forgive them, nor the scumbags in question.

The Boy, the Girl, the Fish and the Spider...

So despite the fact that we had ploughed at least £6000 into their once failing mortgage, and had also paid for the maroon pick-up in the driveway, we were now considered outsiders as far as the Naenudon family were concerned. That really did blow, and I drastically adjusted my opinion of this once seemingly happy Thai family. Although I have more than my fair share of flaws, I've always managed to be able to adjust when necessary, and Jum has the same ability.

'Okay, we go stay Yai Dee and build house.' Almost as if she was suggesting how we would merely spend the afternoon, Jum had made the decision that would change our destiny, albeit in a way that we had yet to learn.

I could see Yai Kit's body language alter drastically as her daughter calmly explained our Plan B. Her eyes started to shift from left to right and back again and I knew there was something wrong. She them waddled off to the back of the house and I could hear her pudgy fingers dialling furiously, quite a lot of numbers it seemed.

Instead of eavesdropping we decided that after a two hour journey in a pretty ramshackle bus, we'd visit the only restaurant in the village for some much needed refreshment. After all, we hadn't exactly been offered any alternative by Yai Kit.

It's amazing how much better the world looks after a cup of hot tea and we must have spent an hour just talking about the past two months. Although life hadn't been a bed of roses, we were the Hall Family, and this Scottish-Thai union was made of far sterner stuff than any outsider could ever fathom. Our time in Fort William, the challenges of coming to terms with my father's dementia and Mum's failing health, combined with the fraught Indian experience, and now this – well, we would deal with anything else that the world wanted to pitch our way. Bring it on!

As we'd ambled back to chez Naenudon we were given a totally unexpected greeting – in fact, I had not experienced such a welcome for years, if ever. Except it wasn't Jum's family, neither were these hosts even human!

Euro and Jelly were two cross-bred mutts that had been resident at 88/8 Ban Mai for at least a decade, and the fine creatures must have remembered our last visit, all of five years back. Perhaps it was because we had always offered them snacks and ensured that their water bowls always had something cool and wet to offer, who knows? But they more than made up for the ignorant old lady's reaction two hours odd earlier.

After the affectionate duo were finally done with us and had sloped off with their snacks, courtesy of Tom, we noticed Yai Kit sitting in a somewhat forlorn state at the front of the open shop front that was a part of the house.

'On... Ma Nee.' She ushered Jum towards her, using her childhood name, and this alone indicated that something was not quite right. In my experience of Yai Kit, she was only nice when she either wanted money or she had screwed up royally – sometimes a combination of the both. So which was this?

Usually I would give my wife some space when she was speaking to her mum, but this – well, I wanted to hear for myself.

Yai Kit spoke in a very hushed tone as she explained an issue that could possibly throw a major spanner in the works. But before she got to the crux of the matter she surprised us by letting us know in no uncertain terms that, in her opinion, Thailand was no place for Tom. How could we even think of taking him away from the UK, that place with so many positives? The schooling, the safety, the great jobs and pretty much everything that Thailand didn't have on offer? – This was Yai Kit's view of the UK, and although I understood her opinion, I knew that this was the precursor for something altogether less straightforward.

Finally, she let us have it, with both barrels.

In 2006 we had sent over £800. This was intended for Yai Dee as total payment for the land, as agreed. Unfortunately Yai Dee had no bank account to speak of, so we sent the funds over to Jum's parent's account instead. We issued strict instructions that this money should be withdrawn and paid to Yai Dee, and in return we would receive the deeds to the land.

Except that this did not happen.

No. What did happen was just becoming apparent, and it was extremely hard to swallow.

Although we had not visited Thailand since that holiday back in 2006, Jum's sister would come over every year. The arrival of the money had coincided with Hoi's visit and she

The Boy, the Girl, the Fish and the Spider...

was very interested in the whole arrangement. According to Yai Kit, Hoi had decided that we shouldn't have the land, and that instead the money would be split between her and her other two sisters, Goon and Ooi.

Which was very generous of her – in fact, I was surprised that she didn't keep the lot for herself!

Yai Dee had not received a penny and, in her eyes, we had probably thought better of the whole real estate deal.

As Jum took this information on board, I could feel her anger and disbelief starting to rise. Not for the first time, her sister had shafted us and we had been made fools of for the umpteenth time.

The fact that Hoi had been introduced to my then-best friend and had managed to flee Ban Mai for the idyllic country about which Yai Kit had waxed lyrically earlier on seemed to have no bearing on the way that she, and he, had treated us after their union.

Sorry, I am kind of getting side tracked here, so I'll cut to the chase and get back to the remaining Siamese fighting fish crew shortly!

So the money had been passed over to three pairs of greedy little mitts, and now we were starting to think about a plan C – or even D!

Then I witnessed a transformation in my wife that was very new to me, and I stood back as she assumed control of the situation in a way any Brigadier or Admiral would have been proud of. Although her voice never became a shout, it did take on a tone that both amazed and scared the life out of me.

Tom and I and the two dogs looked on, wide eyed, as Jum explained how we rolled and how things were going to be.

She knew that her elder sister, Goon, held the purse strings here in Ban Mai, as her younger sibling Hoi did in the UK. The money had better be back in our hands before the end of the day, or there would be repercussions!

Nobody doubted this tiny daughter of Thailand, because when my wife moved out of her comfort zone and stepped up to the plate, she meant business!

Before the conversation had ended, Goon pulled up in her brand new pickup and her offspring, Pang and Spark came over, looking more bemused than anything else. Judging by

Bangkok to Ben Nevis Backwards!

their reactions something very bad had happened that we were yet to learn about, but it wouldn't be very long before that was revealed.

Suffice it to say, by 4 o'clock we had the fifty thousand baht and had moved our dust-stained suitcases the 400 yards or so to Yai Dee's house, where the land was paid for and all was settled once more.

So, back to the fish, all two of them.

Pang and her cronies were notable by their absence for the next two days and, as plans for the house build got under way, I moved on from that unpleasant experience. Tom was very attentive to both of the fish, and he also had become rather attached to Godzilla, the enormous Golden Orb Weaver. We had even picked out a lovely mango tree for her release in the near future, with plenty of food available and maybe even a potential mate or two lurking.

Yai Dee seemed to know an awful lot about house building, and pretty soon we were drawing up plans for our new residence. The price of materials and labour in Isaan had meant that we could have a house that would set you back at least £300,000 in the UK, for less than £10,000 here – and that was including the price of the land!

She was extremely strong willed and despite the fact that it would be our house, Yai Dee wanted the final say on how the whole building would look, as though it would affect the resale price of her own dwelling – bless her!

Of course, we needed no council planning permission and I was really looking forward to the whole event. Once the house was built I would start looking for a job in earnest. Can you imagine doing things this way back home? Although I was missing my parents, particularly after the way we had left them, I could enthusiastically see the potential of living here in Thailand.

We also had to get Tom's education back on track, not an easy proposition and one that made me think about my own reasons for coming here in the first place. Was I yet again putting my own pleasures and ambitions before my wife and son's?

You see, as a child I had lived in Singapore, Malaysia, Wales, South Africa and England over the span of just thirteen years, and I had turned out fine. Well, almost.

The Boy, the Girl, the Fish and the Spider...

Dad had been in the armed forces, and after meeting his sweetheart in South Uist all those years ago, they set off for a globetrotting adventure with three young kids in tow. But all of those countries had something in common; they had a decent education system in place. Our first choice, India, also boasted a fine academic infrastructure. But Thailand?

I kept pushing this topic to the back of my mind, thinking that it would be alright in the end.

Amidst the comings and goings of the newly appointed house-building crew, I almost didn't notice the reappearance of Pang and Spark, and their cohorts. By now I had got their number and had explained to Tom to be on the lookout for them, especially as far as the fish were concerned. He had wisely suggested that we return the watery duo to the shop until our house was built. This mature and selfless decision made me feel proud because I knew Tom was growing into a far better person than I turned out to be.

But the day before we were to take the fighting fish back to the shop, all hell was to break loose once more.

I called Tom to the veranda and as I was about to warn him about the incoming threat we both looked on in disbelief as Pang, looking directly as us, poured something into the flowerpot. By the time I reached it, the two fish were already floating on the surface. The bleach had made short work of the poor guys and I was beginning to consider doing serious prison time on their behalf.

She had won.

'It only fish!' she sneered, and flounced off with her minions not far behind.

I looked at my son and saw tears streaming down his face. He looked at me and said, 'So much for Buddha!'

I had to smile because it was true; Thais were supposed to be devout Theravada Buddhists and were not meant to harm living creatures except for food. Pang had broken quite a few Buddhist rules, along with three of four of the Ten Commandments, in less than ten seconds!

It was then that I realised the little buggers had moved over to the veranda, and their attentions were now focussed on Godzilla. Pang was shaking the sweet jar for all she was worth, and as Tom reached her she flung it into the fence just beside the road.

He jumped over the small veranda wall and quickly

opened up the lid. What happened next will stay with me for the rest of my days.

He reached into the jar, and as he carefully withdrew his hand I could see the rather crumpled shape of the Golden Orb Weaver; clearly she had had better days but was very much alive. The group of miscreants looked on, open-mouthed, as Tom marched their way. The screams may well have woken the dead, because I could have sworn I heard Jum's deceased father chuckling away up above.

Tom chased the miscreants and finally cornered the evil Pang, who was by now bawling her eyes out. She seemed powerless as Tom held Godzilla inches away from her face. Just as I thought he was about to force the harmless yet gigantic arachnid into this cruel child's face, he pulled back and skipped towards me.

We relocated Godzilla into our soon-to-be garden, and when we reached the veranda we encountered a furious looking Goon, who looked as if she was about to explode.

'I've got this, Dad,' Tom whispered, and as he shot a skewed smile towards Goon and the quivering Pang, he uttered: 'It's only a bloody spider!'

Life in Thailand was going to be many things, but boring was certainly not one of them!

The Boy, the Girl, the Fish and the Spider…

Our House… well, some of it!

Chapter 8

How These People Roll

One of my weaknesses, and also Jum's, is that we tend to be a little too soft and never seem to learn from our mistakes. Okay, I'm mainly talking about when dealing with those people who are born to take advantage.

So let's look at Jum's family. Not a great track record to be honest, and we always ended up being taken for a ride. I've already spoken about the land issue, thanks to the 3 Bitches, but that doesn't even come close to what happened next.

A few days after the fish and spider floor show, I could sense that Yai Dee had started to get bored of us living under her roof. Our house was still being built, and I could not wait for the day that we finally moved in. Don't get me wrong, I appreciated her hospitality and all, but this was a tiny house and the two not-so-young lovers probably needed their personal space back.

The only thing holding up the builder's progress was Yai Dee herself, who insisted on overseeing literally every swing of the hammer – and she wasn't slow in coming forward as far as criticism was concerned, either. We lost two complete teams of builders thanks to her vile tongue, and I had long since given up trying to influence the way that our house would be built; she knew best apparently.

We'd tried looking at local schools for Tom, and I had also been to look at a few with a view to starting my teaching career. Neither exercise was entirely fruitful and we'd decided to wait until the house was built, most probably rent it out, and then move to the city for better prospects. We'd kept this plan quiet from Yai Dee because we weren't

Bangkok to Ben Nevis Backwards!

sure how she would take to strangers living next door.

One lovely morning, after going to the local temple for prayers, I was starting to speculate how she'd react to this news when I heard a wild screaming that told me I'd not have to worry any more. She already knew!

Jum had been speaking to her friends in Kalasin about schools and housing, and Yai Leeuw had been eavesdropping. She'd reported directly back to her surly paymaster, and all hell was being unleashed. Although I had a basic understanding of Thai and knew more than my fair share of swear words, there were dozens of new ones suddenly ringing in my ears on that peaceful Isaan morning. Even the builders had stopped their work to listen – not that they usually needed an excuse!

Jum was forced to listen as Yai Dee called her all the names under the sun, and a few that came from a far darker place. She then started picking up stones and throwing them in Jum's direction. As one of them hit my wife square on the forehead, I intervened and shoved Yai Dee hard enough to knock her over. She then tried to pick another stone up, more like a rock, and had a mad look in her eye that scares me to this day.

She never got the chance to throw it because Tom stood in between us, and one of the builders restrained her.

'Phil, we have to leave!' Jum was stating the obvious but within twenty minutes we'd removed all traces of our belongings and relocated to her mother's house. Bizarrely, Jum and Yai Kit were on better terms and if anything, this had made their relationship a little less shaky.

I was furious, and what made matters worse was the fact that I was due to fly to Bangkok a few days later for a four-week TEFL training course. I'd already paid about £700 for this but now I felt as if I needed to stay.

As we discussed this potential nightmare, Jum's phone rang and her face turned from a frown into a beaming smile as she shared the news. 'Megan is at the airport!'

Amidst all the chaos we had yet again forgotten about the fourth family member. We'd planned to house her at Yai Dees, but that wasn't going to happen now. Yai Kit wasn't a dog lover, but despite this she had Jelly and Euro, both Thai mongrels whom we loved.

Two hours later myself and Jum were at Kohn Kaen

airport in the cargo section. It had been nearly two months and the bill was horrendous, but we didn't care. Maybe now we could start to function as a family once more!

Here was my latest list:

1. Collect Megan (obviously)
2. Find somewhere to live in Kalasin city
3. Job and School for me and Tom
4. Sell or rent our house once built

It was more and more obvious that I hadn't really thought things through – plus I still had to sort out our bank card issues with our UK bank. There was less than £1,000 in my account by now, and I still had to pay the builders.

My thoughts were interrupted by an approaching airport cargo vehicle beeping its horn. The side doors swung open and there she was – our darling Megan!

She instantly recognised me, and the weirdest bark was emitted as I approached her and waited for the airport employee to open the cargo case we'd bought back in the UK.

She darted straight past me and into her mistress's arms and I looked on as the mutual admiration club made up for lost time.

Her voice had all but disappeared thanks to a mixture of stress and barking too many times, but apart from this, Megan Hall was in good health and we drove back to Ban Mai Chai with the missing piece of the Hall family jigsaw puzzle finally intact.

Yai Kit was non-plussed when we introduced Megan to her, but the family dogs were quite friendly with Megan and before long she was following Jum everywhere she went, just like old times!

It was New Years' Eve and I couldn't wait to say goodbye to 2011. A somewhat bizarre 365 days and although most of it hadn't panned out too well, I really hoped that the next set would be a little kinder to us all. I decided that I had better pack for my trip to Bangkok.

We didn't bother celebrating the New Year, and the next day I rose early to prepare for my flight and onward journey. I had already booked a hotel room in Bangkok for seven days, and would look for cheaper lodgings after a few days into the teaching course. The school term ended in March and this was the best time to look for a teaching job.

This would be the first time that I'd be alone in Thailand since being married, and I'd be lying if I said I wasn't just a little bit excited. I really hoped that everything would run smoothly back at the ranch – surely they could behave until I came back, couldn't they?

My Brother in law, Lot, drove me to the airport and I said a slightly tearful goodbye to Tom and Jum before climbing into the old pickup. We'd bought this for Jum's father about seven years ago, and since his demise nobody had even cleaned the poor vehicle.

Less than four hours later I was in Bangkok and had checked into my new home for the next week or so. I called Jum and she wasted no time in telling me to look after myself and to stay away from any bars or massage parlours... as if?! How could she even think that I would be interested in this seedy side of Thai culture? The very cheek of the woman!

Then she went on to say that Yai Dee had moved the boundaries separating our land from hers, and had reclaimed around 20 metres of it!

I was furious but warned my wife not to do anything hasty. In fact, she should wait until I returned because that old bag would have done this deliberately to provoke Jum into kicking off. Yai Dee had a history of violence and rumour has it that this evil old witch had previous form for stabbing people!

Of course, my advice would be ignored; it usually was.

My hotel was based on Sukhumvit road, a lively tourist area, so I took a shower and headed out for a few refreshing beers. When I say a few, I mean about seven or eight; I kind of lost count, and enjoyed this rare slice of freedom.

The next day I awoke with a mild hangover, and for the first time in three months I pulled on a pair of smart trousers and a shirt and tie. By the time I had reached the MRT station, I was sweating like a stuck pig. Jesus it was hot, probably close to 40 degrees and not even 8 a.m. – how would I cope when I started teaching?

Thankfully the train was nicely air conditioned and I played Spot The Foreigner, as I soon realised that most of the travellers were Thai and they seemed to be copying their British counterparts on the London tube. If you've ever taken the tube, you'll know what I mean when I say that to a man, or woman, each of these commuters was engrossed in the daily newspaper, and conversation was non-existent.

Same-same, but different.

Following the printed instructions, I changed trains at Siam and hopped on the Bang Wa line before jumping off at Si Lom station. The entire journey had only lasted twelve minutes, and the TEFL offices were just over the road from the station.

As I reached the front door of the offices I felt the vibration of my phone in my back pocket, and delayed my entrance to answer the call. The receptionist briefly looked up from her breakfast without making eye contact, and quickly went back to chowing down as I heard my son's frantic voice on the other end of the line.

'Dad, Mum has been stabbed!'

'Tom, calm down and tell me what happened?'

My son breathed deep, then told me that despite my own advice, Jum had gone to Yai Dee's house early this morning with several family members, including Bitch Numbers 1 and 2. There she had physically uprooted the boundary posts and returned them to their original positions.

I could tell what would have happened next.

Yep, Yai Dee had then appeared with her girlfriend and a huge shouting match had ensued. At the peak of this verbal battle, Yai Dee had marched straight up to my wife, produced a large machete from out of nowhere and had aimed a strike directly at Jum's head.

Jum had apparently raised her left arm and managed the block the strike. The machete had gone deep into her arm just below the elbow joint. Yai Dee then twisted the machete until the bone cracked.

Not a single family member had stepped in, and as my wife fell to the ground her assailant calmly removed the blade and returned to her house, lesbian in tow.

'Tom, where is Mum now?'

He said that he alone had arranged for Jum to be taken to the nearest hospital, and that was where he was calling

from. She had lost a lot of blood but was now stable, thank God.
A sudden voice made me look up, startled. 'Are you Philip Hall?'
A middle-aged European man was watching me with a concerned look on his face.
Somehow, I managed to speak. 'My wife has been stabbed, I have to go...'
Without waiting for an answer I turned around and returned to my hotel. I tried in vain to get a refund for the unused nights, packed up and jumped into a taxi. I'd probably lose the money from the TEFL course and more besides. Why, oh why, did this have to happen right now?
Of course, when an emergency happened I usually started blaming people before I calmed down. Despite the terrible nature of this scenario, I reverted to type and cursed my bad luck. It was only when the plane had landed in Kohn Kaen that the full force of the attack hit me.
My wife could have died, had she not reacted so quickly!
Then I started to blame myself.
Why hadn't we stayed in India? Why hadn't we stayed in the UK?
I began to piece together the whole sorry set of circumstances that had led to this near-tragedy.

- The debts – my fault.
- Selling our home to pay the debts – also my fault.
- Choosing to come to India – my fault.
- Giving up on India – my fault.
- Coming to Thailand – my fault.

Okay, it wasn't me who swung the machete, neither was it my fault that dear old Dad had Dementia, but everything else – my fault.
How could I make everything right? So far it was all losses and practically zero wins.
Hang on, I did manage to get Jum's card unblocked – that was some kind of win, surely?
It had taken a three hour phone call and plenty of sweet talk but, by Buddha, I had done it!

I hailed a taxi and during the two hour journey to the Kalasin municipal hospital, I had plans and lists going through my mind like never before. This tragic event had put a hold on everything, and it struck me how much I loved my dear wife. What would we do without her? Jum had been the rock in my life that I so badly needed.

As the taxi ploughed through the Isaan countryside I noticed the rice fields and saw that they were a hive of activity, with hundreds of labourers hunched over picking up the harvest. Jum had been born from this very stock, and it was the same people who had very nearly ended her short life.

Then I started to feel anger and hatred towards her auntie; I had given this woman the benefit of the doubt so far, but that had been a big mistake. Once I established that Jum was okay, I would do my utmost to deal with Yai Dee. I would give my all to this mission, because this vile woman deserved punishment and she was going to regret her actions for the rest of her life!

Finally we arrived at Kalasin municipal hospital. There were dozens of people sitting in the Outpatients area, and I noticed one poor fellow had what could only be described as a six foot metal pole protruding from his skull! He had a buddy who was holding the object, and I could only imagine how that had happened. Thailand was not at all Health and Safety conscious, and this hospital bore testament to that fact.

Apparently Jum was on the 3rd floor, and I called Tom's mobile for directions. A few minutes later I saw my son rushing towards me; I could see that he had been crying. As we hugged he told me that Jum's family hadn't even come to the hospital with her – in fact, Bitch Number 2 had made a joke about how overly serious Tom was being about the whole attack!

This was the very same woman to whom we had given 30,000 Thai baht a few years earlier to set up a business with her boyfriend! (I say 'given' because when you lend money in Thailand, you may as well consider it a gift because you'll never see it again.) The business had been quite successful – until the police had become involved.

Unbeknownst to us, The Bitch and her boyfriend had used the funds to buy a shedload of methamphetamine

Bangkok to Ben Nevis Backwards!

tablets and set themselves up as the premier drug dealers in Ban Mai Chai and the surrounding villages. They were quite the entrepreneurs right up until the point where they tried flogging their wares to an undercover cop. Her boyfriend went to prison; this was at a time when the government was cracking down on criminal behaviour. We then received another call for help because if he didn't come up with 20,000 Thai baht in the next week, he'd probably be jailed for twenty-five years. Thailand does not muck about when it comes to sentencing, but their law enforcers are fairly open to the odd financial deal.

Of course, being the softies that we were, we dug deep and stumped up once more. So if you were wondering why I had issues with Jum's sisters, hopefully this will clarify things a little!

Now, as we walked into the small hospital room, I could see my wife laid up in bed. She looked as pale as I had ever seen her. The golden skin that had attracted me to Jum in the first place was now looking sallow and unhealthy. She still managed a weak smile, and I did my best not to show my concern.

A few of her old friends were in the room and these good people had been helping Tom look after Jum since her arrival. Family? Nowhere to be seen. Despite their poor track record, I struggled to come to terms with their behaviour.

Jum had lost a lot of blood and had already endured a long operation, during which the surgeon placed a metal pin in her arm to assist the healing. The cut had been so deep that it had pretty much sliced through her bone, and the way that Yai Dee had twisted the machete had snapped the remainder as if it were a twig.

'Have you spoken to the Police yet?' I asked Jum – stupid question, because how could she have? She needed rest, not the added stress that I was creating. But when you have nothing but plans and hope, this type of horrific incident scatters them to the wind, and my head was hurting as a result.

In my heart however, I had one thing in mind.

Revenge.

I didn't even know how yet, but I would make Yai Dee accountable for this murder attempt. It was now my only real objective.

TOM, YAI KIT, PANG AND POO PAP

Of course, in hindsight I should have simply concentrated my efforts on Jum's recovery. I spoke with the doctor, who told me that Jum would eventually get back some use of her arm, but that the healing would take at least six months. We could leave the hospital the next day, but would have to return every day for the next month.

Although the Thai health system is far from perfect, there is one bonus for Thai citizens: whatever medical treatment they may need, the bill will only amount to 30 Thai Baht – about 60 pence. But because Jum was no longer a resident of Thailand, thanks to the cancellation of her ID card by her sister, we would have to pay the full amount for treatment. Jum's bill had already amounted to 10,000 Thai Baht - £200, and was rising on an hourly basis. We shouldn't put a cost on what was potentially lifesaving treatment, but I was determined that somebody else would pay for this, and then some!

In terms of finding somewhere to live, well – thanks to one of Jum's friends, Pla, we had that covered. Pla and Jum were school buddies, and despite the thousands of miles between them they had stayed in touch. It is at times like these when you can count the true friends on the fingers of one hand, and Pla had stepped up to the plate when it mattered. For that, we will always be grateful.

We moved into Pla's house the next day, into a large room with several mattresses and a fan at our disposal. This was to be our home for the next month. They'd even brought Megan over from Ban Mai without any fuss at all.

That evening, settling into bed in our new chambers, I looked round at our battered family and not for the first time wondered – how could I have got it so wrong? Okay, this wasn't all of my fault, but in terms of cause and effect, who else could be blamed?

Wearily, I reached for a pen and paper and laid out the next set of plans, for what they were worth:

1. Speak to police
2. Ensure that Yai Dee gets what is coming to her
3. Sell house, or at least what had been built so far
4. Find somewhere to live
5. School for Tom
6. Job for me

Suddenly, all of the important stuff seemed to have taken a back seat and all I was focusing on was justice.

Except that this was Thailand. Justice was not exactly something we usually associated with this rather exotic and sometimes whacky Kingdom.

I drifted off to sleep, and my dreams were full of old ladies and exceptionally large machetes all flying in my direction.

Chapter 5

WE ARE FAMILY

Have you ever sat down and really thought what 'family' actually means? It seems that in the Western world, family values have all but disappeared in some cases. Marriage is no longer sacred; and whatever happened to sitting down for tea or dinner and chatting about how everyone's day had been?

In Thailand it is different though. Here, family is supposed to be everything, and quite often that is the case. But what happens when two members of the same family have a serious falling out? What side will the family take, and does it even matter who is right and who is wrong?

In the case of the Naenudon family, I was about to find out the answer, whether I liked it or not.

A few days after relocating to Pla's house, we paid a visit to the Kalasin police station to file charges against Yae Dee for attempted murder. Pla came with us, as she knew one of the more senior police officials; in fact, she cut his hair once a month. She was a talented hair dresser, and most of Kalasin's high society (or Hi-So as they say in Thailand) would drop in for their regular dose of gossip and short back and sides.

Once she mentioned his name to the policeman at the front desk, we were soon ushered into an air conditioned office and offered cool water whilst we waited. Khun Paiboon soon appeared and, once the pleasantries had been exchanged, we got down to the reason why we had requested his audience.

Khun Paiboon listened intently and scribbled furiously

as Jum talked him through the events leading up to and including the attack. His expression didn't change once; it was as if Jum were describing a recipe for Tom Yum Goong, he was that animated.

When she finally finished, Khun Paiboon scribbled for another minute and then looked up with a beaming smile. He spoke rapidly and I could only pick up the odd word here and there, but basically, the gist was this:

1. He would issue a warrant for Yae Dee's arrest
2. The local Ban Mai police would then arrest her
3. Witnesses would be called in to verify what happened
4. She would be either charged and sentenced, or fined.

Wait - fined?? As if this was a bloody parking ticket!

Apparently we had the power to choose whether she went to jail or was hit with a fine.

I liked the idea of both punishments being meted out, but apparently they were exclusive.

When we returned from the station we found bitch number one and two waiting for us in the salon. Instead of showing concern for their elder sister, they had faces like thunder and let rip with a stream of expletives so vile that even a passing monk was shaking his head as he scurried out of earshot.

These two women were berating my wife for even thinking of going to the police. After all, this was a family matter and the family would deal with it!

I had real issues with their attitude, and was about to tell them where to go, but Jum stepped up and explained, in her awesome no-nonsense tone, what was going to happen.

They listened but I could sense the hatred building in in them. Just exactly what had Jum done to her sisters to make them quite so hideous?

A few weeks ago, before the fish and spider debacle, we had found out that my wife's name had been removed from the Naenudon home. This was an act of spite from Bitch #3, and the consequences were far reaching. Without her name on the property, Jum couldn't have an ID card. Without an ID card, Jum couldn't work; she couldn't rent a house, a car or a motorbike. She couldn't even renew her Thai passport.

We Are Family

At the time of discovering this, we needed a bank account and in order to open one, you needed... yes, an ID card!

Bitch #2's husband, poor man, was a policeman, and because of this association we'd been able to open a basic account with Bangkok Bank. So long as he would be so kind as to act as a reference, there would be no problem. Except Bitch #2 wanted something in return. Not much, just 10,000 baht, a bottle of Johnny Walker Black Label and a load of cigarettes.

When you consider that 10,000 baht is more than her husband would make in a month, you kind of get the idea of what sort of person she really was. They saw us as cash cows, nothing else.

But money doesn't buy loyalty, and we were finding this out.

They had told Jum that not a single person would bear witness to the attack. Without a witness, there would be no case and we'd be lucky to get a single baht for our troubles.

I wasn't that surprised really, but the enormity of the whole screw-up had finally dawned on me. We'd travelled halfway around the globe to stay with THESE people? Really??

Tom was pretty upset; he wanted to know why his Mum's family were such lowlife. For myself, I needed to get this justice sorted out before we could progress with any other plans.

The next day we travelled to the district police station and we were met with total disinterest. It transpired that several of the officers were old friends of Yai Dee's, imagine that! They advised us that they already knew of the case and would not be pressing charges. They practically laughed us out of the station!

Pla kindly agreed to drive us back to the scene of the crime and I was rather looking forward to confronting the person who had all but destroyed our family. Jum warned me not to do anything violent; she knew I had a temper. But what was the worst that could happen? I knew that if I did harm a hair on her head, there would be a queue of ready witnesses at least a mile long.

So by my thinking, I may as well be hung for a Yai Dee as for a lamb...

Bangkok to Ben Nevis Backwards!

Before the showdown that I had been dreaming about, we stopped off at the family home. Jum was heavily strapped up and as we left the car, her mother looked over and didn't show one ounce of concern. In fact, her face was fairly similar to Bitch Numbers 1 and 2: hatred.

Apparently the news had spread and even the two dogs looked agitated as we endured a stream of abuse that left me in no doubt as to our position in this whole terrible mess: it was all our own fault; if we'd only stayed back in the UK, this would not have happened! – typical Thai logic.

I'd heard stories about when a foreigner and a Thai experienced a road traffic accident; the foreigner would always be blamed because, if he had only stayed in his country, the accident would not have happened. So by this logic, the whole disaster would not have happened had we stayed in UK, or even India for that matter.

But we were family – at least that should count for something, surely?

Apparently not. Yai Dee was also family, and in their eyes she was more important.

I'd had just about enough of this crap, and started walking towards the side road where our house was being built; I wanted to see Yai Dee. Jum tried calling me back, but by now Tom had joined me, and as we left the main road he asked me:

'What are you going to do, Dad?'

I had no idea, but it wasn't going to be very nice.

Then something altogether weird happened.

Have you ever noticed that when the world and his wife are against you, everyone else seems to jump on the bandwagon? We were passing a small field where about twenty children aged between 8 and 15 were having a kick about. They noticed us and stopped their game – we were far more interesting.

'Bok See Da! Bok See Da! Bok See Da!' they all chanted as the mini-pack approached us. They were using the Isaan dialect to call us 'Foreigners'.

The literal translation was actually 'Guava'. The Thai guava has a white flesh that has been compared to our pasty European skin. The term 'Bok' was a very derogatory particle and wasn't exactly what Tom and I wanted to hear right now.

We marched on regardless and just two side roads away from our destination I noticed a large stone whiz past my head. We stopped and another stone, this time larger and closer, smashed onto the road. We were under attack.

I turned around to see if it was the 'would be' footballers but they had returned to their game. As a third stone actually made contact with my leg, I noticed a very strange sight to our left.

Inside a garden, under some large trees, there was a wooden cage. Contained within this cage was a semi-naked man who looked pretty upset. I had the urge to throw the stone back in his direction but Tom stopped me.

'Dad, he's probably crazy, let's go!'

I agreed and within two minutes we had reached Yai Dee's front door.

I noticed the bloody boundary posts had been moved even further back; it seemed our decent-sized garden was now a footpath for termites that had to squeeze themselves into the five or six inches of land around our house.

As I knocked heavily on the door I also realised that all building work had stopped; our industrious workforce was nowhere to be seen.

After a few minutes it was clear that nobody was going to answer our knocking, so we went round the back and I looked through the kitchen screen door. Either Yai Dee was hiding somewhere or she was simply not home.

We walked back to the family home and Jum told us she had just discovered that Yai Dee had taken off the previously day. Apparently the police had advised her to 'do one' and she had followed their instructions. Jum's mother had explained to her the way that things were going to be.

'Phil, nobody will help us!'

So the family had ruled in favour of the old cow who had now absconded and here we were again, at the bottom of the Naenudon food chain. But it wasn't all bad news; they had agreed to pay the grand sum of 50,000 Thai baht to help with the situation.

Bitch #2 also had some 'good' news. She could sell our partially built house. The price had yet to be agreed, but she knew someone who didn't mind living next to a machete-wielding old banshee – and obviously we couldn't go and live there now.

Bangkok to Ben Nevis Backwards!

We'd spent around 200,000 Thai baht on materials, labour and land.

Jum said that we'd think about it, and Pla suggested that we make our excuses and leave.

A little while after we left Ban Mai Chai, Jum quietly sobbed and asked nobody in particular why her family hated her so much? Even Pla was reduced to tears, and I felt more anger than I had thought possible as I tried in vain to comfort my wife.

Over the next few weeks we did our best to return to normality. Tom was getting Thai lessons every evening and I started to look for work. We found a small townhouse and after about three weeks staying at Pla's house, we finally said goodbye to her kind hospitality and moving into a two-up-two-down in a little lane called Moo Ban Mai Thai.

The neighbours were a curious bunch, and within an hour of our moving in a small welcoming party appeared and invited themselves in. They were mainly interested in why a white man with a Thai wife and a 'luk krung' (half-blood) had decided to move into their neighbourhood.

They also asked about Jum's injury, and after twenty minutes or so they had brought round enough food for a street party. You see, Thai people aren't all like Jum's family. They listened in amazement as Jum re-enacted the machete incident and I could tell that they were dumbstruck when they heard about the treatment we had to endure afterwards.

We slept well that night, and when I awoke I saw that Jum was already up. I heard the familiar voices of Bitches #1 and #2.

About ten of Jum's extended family stood outside our new home, and they looked as if they meant business. Apparently it was time for them to pay the piper, and I looked on as Jum counted the money. On top of the 50,000 Thai baht from Yai Dee, there was another 150,000 for our 'home'. This was closure, and we would just have to deal with it. Although it was better than nothing, I knew that we had been taken for a ride once more.

Jum asked where her mother was; they explained that her Diabetes-related illness had flared up and she was currently in hospital. Jum looked concerned, and handed over 2,000 Thai baht from our little nest egg.

I couldn't believe it! Despite being treated like a piece of detritus, my wife was now showing the very compassion that had made me fall for her all those years ago.

Her kindness was met with a mixture of disbelief and mild scorn. Bitch #1 must have sensed some weakness, and seized this opportunity to ask for a short term loan.

'Ee Kwai – Bai! *(Get lost, you water buffalo* – only in harsher terms!)' Jum made short work of the cheeky request and I laughed inwardly as the rest of the throng sniggered at the spurned sister.

As we turned and went back into the townhouse, I wondered how she could still be anything but cold towards her mother. I guess she had something that her sisters probably never did. Jum was kind and honest, two attributes that equated to weakness in some people's eyes. At that moment, I loved her more than anything else in the world.

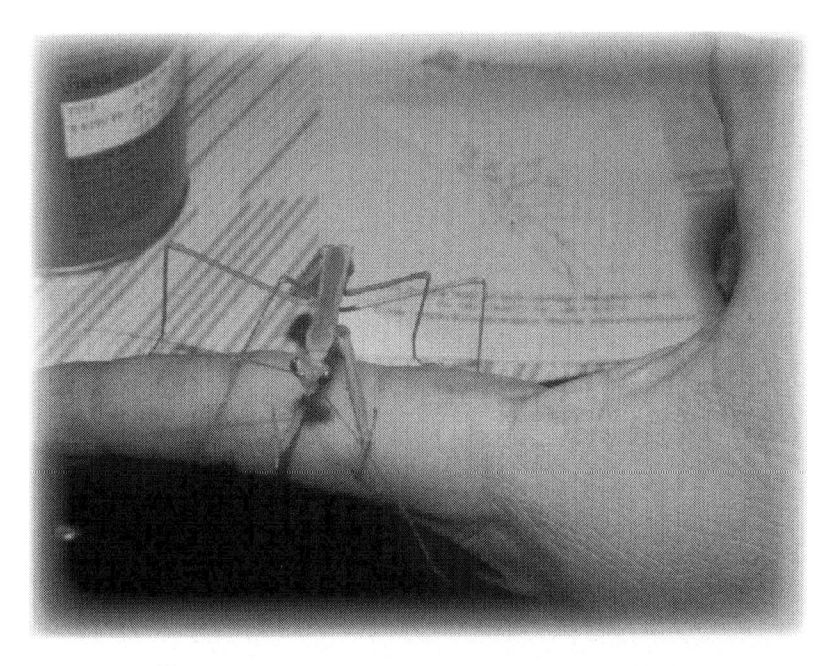

THIS CREATURE HAS MORE INTEGRITY THAN THE REST OF JUM'S FAMILY COMBINED

Chapter 10

The People's Democratic Republic of Laos

After a few days in our new home we realised that our visas were about to expire and we'd have to sort a trip out pretty quickly. If you come to Thailand without any sort of visa, you'll get a 30-day stamp, which can be extended by a certain time if you visit your local immigration office. Somehow we'd managed to get an extra two months, but this would run out in three days from now. I suggested to Jum that we travel up to Vientiane, the capital of Laos, to get a 60-day tourist visa. (Even though Jum was a Thai national, with as yet no ID card she had to rely on her UK passport and therefore must have a visa.)

We'd never been to Laos and it would be a welcome break from the rubbish that we'd endured recently. Our funds were being eaten into, and even the money we'd clawed back from the house sale and machete attack wasn't going to last long. The problem was that we had no means of income yet, with three bored people and a little white dog tending to spend money for amusement.

We'd bought a small red motorbike and had started to explore the city of Kalasin indepth, Although the little house was okay, it had only a tiny courtyard at the front, and Jum yearned for a house with a garden. We decided that once we returned from Laos, we'd look into renting a more suitable place.

Jum still had no ID card and the only way forward, as far as we could see, was to find some old documents that were hopefully back home in Roy Bridge. I'd left some suitcases with our photographs and other memorabilia in Mum and

Dad's loft. Amongst these were various official Thai papers that we'd kept; perhaps one of them would be sufficient for my wife to be reissued her ID card.

She needed an official birth certificate, because the copy that had been stored at her folks' house in Ban Mai Thai had mysteriously 'disappeared'. I had called Mum a few days earlier and the conversation had been difficult, to say the least.

'I'm not sure we can get in the loft any more, dear,' Mum explained earnestly.

She asked if I would like to speak to Dad but when I did, he had absolutely no idea who I was. This broke my heart even more.

I said goodbye to Mum and she promised to try and send the envelope full of Thai documents over. She'd also found my wedding band and would pop that in too.

At the end of that particular phone call I felt pretty isolated. Both of our families were either away with the fairies or were hell bent on making our lives hell. What could we do? I'd given up on revenge – what was the point? The only way I could see of moving forward was to do our best to be happy and forget that these people, with the exception of my parents, had ever existed. I had spent a lot of time hating these people, and even more wondering why they had treated us so shabbily.

So a little trip to the People's Democratic Country of Laos could be just what the family doctor ordered.

The very next day, outside of the Kalasin terminal, we caught a minibus which took us to the city of Udon Thani. Here we stopped for noodles and some refreshing mango juice. Megan was being looked after by the vets, a kind pair of sisters who seemed to actually like dogs – something of a rarity in these parts.

Megan hadn't really enjoyed Thailand so far; compared to life back home it was pretty restrictive for the poor little Westie. It was near impossible to walk her due to the lack of open spaces and the concentration of stray dogs that seemed to plague every Thai city. So instead of the traditional walk, we had taken to setting off on the little motorbike. I'd be steering us whilst Jum would be at the back, with Megan squeezed in between us. She absolutely loved this little routine. We'd drive around the city centre and past the street food stalls, where she'd sniff like mad as the heady aromas passed over our heads. Every evening at precisely 6 p.m., Megan would be waiting by the motorcycle, and if we were just a minute late she'd come looking for us. We soon understood that she'd not be messed about!

Now, as we left Udon Thani, I was starting to realise that most Thai cities looked pretty much alike. This place had a population of around 400,000 and was very similar to Kalasin. Nong Khai was our next stop, and at least this border town really had something about it. We had decided to stay here for the night and do the border crossing the next day.

The whole visa process typically took about 24 hours, and as we kicked back for the evening I asked Jum how she was feeling about our trip so far. Of course I meant the whole shebang, not this little excursion.

'Phil, I worry, I worry a lot.'

Jum's concern was, as usual, not for her own well-being but for our son. Tom seemed to be having a good time, but his education was starting to suffer. Okay, he could speak basic Thai and could even read and write a little of it, but that wasn't really enough.

A week earlier we had visited all of the schools in Kalasin and had eventually picked Kalasin Pittayasan as the place for Tom to continue his schooling. KPS was a huge school, over 5000 students and 300 teachers – more like a little city than an educational establishment. They had a decent looking MEP – Mini English Program – where English is taught as a second language, plus Maths, IT, Science were also in our mother tongue. This part of the school had air conditioned classrooms, and there were no more than 30 students in each one.

In contrast, the rest of the school had anything up to 60 per class, no air conditioning and probably way less discipline. I mean, how could a single teacher control such a huge amount of students?

Little was I to know, but I would be finding out in the not too distant future!

Unlike most of the rest of KPS, the students in MEP had to pay around 20,000 Thai Baht per term. Although this only equated to just over £1000 per year, it was a hefty

Bangkok to Ben Nevis Backwards!

enough sum to dissuade all except the more wealthy Thai families from placing their little darlings into the MEP experience.

Tom was due to start his own KPS adventure a few weeks after we returned from Laos. For myself, well – I still didn't have a teaching job, and my aborted TEFL course certainly didn't help matters. Little wonder that my wife worried.

So, back to Nong Khai...

The town itself was nestled on the banks of the Mekhong River, one of the most famous waterways in the whole of Asia. Some 4,350 kilometres long and way over a mile wide, the Mekong supports literally millions – if not billions – of life forms, including plenty of Thais and Laotians. It also provided a very handy border for the two countries.

Laos and Thailand had many similarities, but in terms of technology and other modern nuances there were at least forty or fifty years between them.

The region where we lived, Isaan, was connected to Laos inextricably because of the border and the language. Although Nong Khai was part of Thailand, it was clear that Laos was the main flavour here and the contrast to places like Udon Thani, and even Kalasin, were refreshing. There were practically no high-rise buildings here, and even the traffic was more chilled out.

The three of us travelled around the town in a three-wheeled tuk-tuk. We stopped off at a few markets as we acted like tourists for the first time since we'd arrived in Thailand. The guest house was very groovy, and listed as the only Boutique hotel in Nong Khai.

We weren't overly sure if the 'B word' was apt, but the place was certainly cute and the owner, a local artist, insisted on hosting us for the evening meal. As we munched on fresh line-caught catfish and baked mussels, we looked across the river to Laos, and the amazing sunset was all that was needed to wrap up one of the most relaxing evenings the Hall family had experienced for years. In fact, I was starting to warm to the idea of upping sticks and coming up here to live! But I also knew that after a while, Nong Khai would probably become run of the mill and just too small to pique our collective interests for too long.

We rose early and by 8 a.m. we were at the border, queuing up for entry into Laos. We'd get a one-week visa

The People's Democratic Republic of Laos

stamp in our passports, which was more than enough time to sort out the Thai visa process.

Whilst Jum and Tom sat and waited for our numbers to be called, I found a currency exchange booth to swap my Thai baht for Laotian kip. It was a tiny little currency and a single baht was worth over 200 kip. This would make the bartering a little tricky, as I was still thinking in pounds sterling when buying products in Thai baht.

There was no queue at the booth. I handed over 10,000 Thai baht to the teller and asked for the equivalent in Laotian kip.

At this point, something very strange happened. He explained that they had run out of currency – whilst folding up my 10,000 Thai baht and slipping it into his shirt pocket.

I had heard stories of a dodgy exchange booth on the Thai side of the Friendship Bridge before, and this must be the culprit. Just my luck!

He then tried to pull the wooden shutter down and just before he managed to do so, I grabbed the bottom and used all of my strength to lift it back up. The little bugger started shouting, and before I knew it there was a small crowd of people around us.

He then decided to be brave; he exited the booth and started pushing me for all he was worth. I suppose that this tactic had worked once, somewhere, but the fact that I had handed over a decent wedge of money made me pissed off enough to retaliate in kind.

Usually, if you got into a fight in Thailand with a Thai, the chances were that you would be outnumbered within seconds, but I had sucked up enough crap from Thailand by way of Jum's family to abandon any kind of concern for my own safety. As he came towards me with flailing arms, somewhat like a crazed amphibious octopus, I side-stepped and grabbed him firmly around the neck.

God knows what my next move was going to be but before I could do any more damage I heard a familiar voice ringing through my ears.

'Philip! Stop!'

Indeed, Jum had heard some commotion, and had guessed that I was probably the root cause!

I stopped in my tracks, mid-strangle, and released the thieving little toe rag.

After explaining to Jum what had gone on, she demanded that the man remove the cash from his shirt pocket. To my surprise, he was more scared of her than me, and within seconds he had handed it over, not to me but to my Boss.

The assembled throng soon lost interest and within twenty minutes we were over the border and heading towards our Laotian lodgings. As we drove through Vientiane I noticed a distinct difference in the architecture, and once I'd noted at least two shops with signs depicting them as *boulangeries,* I remembered that Laos was once a French colony. This trip was nothing if not eye opening, if occasionally for the wrong reasons!

I'd booked us into a riverside hotel, and even this looked more like something from a Marcel Carne movie than an Asian flop house. The staff were more than polite, and I was amazed to note that our room actually looked even better than the photos depicted on the Agoda website. The view over the Mekong River was amazing; even though the tide was out, the vibrant mid-morning sun was reflecting from the glistening sands. The effect was breathtaking.

Our itinerary was fairly tight because we needed to be queuing outside the gates before 8 a.m. and I'd heard there was always a mad dash once they opened. We needed photocopies of our Passport main pages and three colour photographs, plus plenty of supporting evidence. For this visa, we just needed to show that we had an address and even though we'd managed to wrangle the rental agreement without Jum having an ID card, I was a little worried that the immigration people would probe deeper.

Tom and Jum crashed out on the balcony sun loungers while I popped down to the reception to see if they had a photocopier I could use. Historically, I'd almost always run into problems when trying to get something simple, yet important, carried out successfully in this type of scenario. However, today was an exception and less than five minutes later I was back in our room with all the photocopies I needed, plus a few more besides.

I got my head down for an hour or two, and after our synchronised snoring session ended we arose. Because the weather was fairly cool, we decided to take a stroll along the banks of the Mekong and possibly take in a few sights.

So far, Laos was comparing favourably to its larger

The People's Democratic Republic of Laos

brother and I was struck by the serenity of the place, as well as the large number of saffron-robed monks who seemed to be everywhere we looked. Although I've never been remotely interested in photography, I wished that I'd had both the skills and equipment to take full advantage of this beautiful city and the surrounding scenery. For now, my camera phone would have to suffice and I sat down on the steps leading to the riverside whilst Jum and Tom walked across the river bed towards the Thai border. There were plenty of people doing exactly the same, so I left them to it and simply relaxed whilst drinking in the sheer serenity of Vientiane.

It wasn't long before my peace was interrupted. I looked up as I heard a soft male voice aimed in my direction; 'Hi Mista, are you alone? Do you want a friend?'

The twenty-something Laotian man was smiling, his hand outstretched. I replied in the negative for both requests and he eventually got the message. I'd long since been able to spot a scammer, and even though there was a chance that this fellow was simply a student wishing to practice his English, I really could not be bothered to indulge him. By the time Jum and Tom had returned I had been approached at least a dozen times –mainly by young men or women; each time they had received the famous Phil Hall cold shoulder.

We walked on and eventually found a French restaurant, where I declared we'd take a late lunch. The food was amazing; even Jum was impressed by the bouillabaisse and freshly baked French bread that was served up. The bill was reasonable and I decided to splash out by leaving a tip.

Although the Laotian Kip wasn't easy to fathom, I was pretty sure that they'd be delighted with their bonus. I left the pile of notes on the tip plate and we were on our way.

Less than a minute later I could hear footsteps and turned around to see an exasperated waiter chasing us up the side street.

'Mister! Mister! Your bill!'

As I started to explain that he could keep the change it dawned on me that I had royally screwed up. Instead of leaving what I thought was about £15 in Kip, I'd actually left closer to £1.50! No wonder he was doing his best Usain Bolt impression! Red-faced I handed over the correct amount and all was well in sleepy Vientiane once more.

Bangkok to Ben Nevis Backwards!

We spent the rest of the day lazing around the swimming pool and when it was approaching 7 p.m. I noticed hundreds of people gravitating towards the riverside. We joined them, to witness one of the most beautiful sunsets imaginable. For now, life was good for the Hall family, and I hoped that we had finally turned a corner.

After a decent night's sleep, we ate a surprisingly authentic English breakfast and made our way to the embassy for our visa application.

As the taxi turned the corner of Avenue Kaysone Phomvihane, I groaned as I took in the massive queue that had already formed outside the Thai embassy. It must have been a good 400 metres long! As we trudged to the end of this human gridlock I noticed the sheer variety of visa applicants who made up the queue. Backpackers were probably the majority, usually twenty-somethings with the obligatory tie-dyed shirts and sandals. There were plenty of well-dressed European men too, who I guessed were teachers looking for their non-immigration B stamps. I'd probably be joining them soon and wondered how stressful that particular process would prove to be.

After an hour or so we heard the gates open and the queue started to lurch forward slowly but surely. After a few minutes we halted, and I realised that we were being let into the embassy in waves.

After another 30 minutes and about five waves later we had reached the Holy Grail; just as they opened once more, a huge man in tight shorts and a Singha beer singlet appeared out of nowhere and shoved his way in front of us. I really despise queue jumpers, but by now I just wanted to get my family in and out of this place and back in the hotel in time for some lunch without further ado.

Jum had other ideas, and as the man-mountain wobbled passed us she literally threw herself in front of him. It was similar to a Shetland pony trying to stop a Shire horse with a draft wagon behind it. I shouted in vain but it was too late; both went crashing to the ground.

Herr Giant Haystacks was non-plussed, but before he could get a word of German (or perhaps Dutch) out, Jum was back on her feet and had read him the riot act. He looked at me sheepishly and I just smiled as we circumnavigated his prone body and made our way to the main building. I wondered if Jum's knack of standing up for herself and for the greater good was the reason her family held her in such low esteem? God only knows, but I for one was glad to be on her side!

The whole process wasn't too bad, and once we'd submitted our forms and documents we were told to come back the following afternoon.

The rest of our visa run went without a hitch, so instead of spending the next night in Nong Khai we decided to get the bus direct to Kalasin. We picked up Megan, who was practically doing back flips when we arrived at the vets. The cost for housing our little dog was less than £2; back in the UK we'd have been looking at 30 or 40 times that amount.

After a day squashed back into our little townhouse I decided that we needed to get a larger place – only made more pressing when we discovered what our neighbours were up to.

A middle-aged couple, whom we'd secretly named Don and Pauline, after our old neighbours back in Wallingford, at first had appeared to be totally normal, but after a few weeks I noticed that something weird was going on. Almost every evening without fail, Don would rock up on his motorbike and there would be a tuk-tuk in tow. The three-wheeler would usually be loaded to the brim with all kinds of appliances: widescreen TVs, PCs, kitchen-related gadgets... all on their way to Chez D&P.

A few days later a random family would appear and, after lots of shouting and no little gnashing of teeth, they'd depart with most of the booty back in their possession.

Don and Pauline were loan sharks.

So I had very little interest in living next to them. I could imagine something major kicking off before too long, and the fact that most Thai households were in possession of a firearm made up my mind that moving was in our best interests.

We soon found a large house with a huge garden, the whole place enclosed within an eight-foot wall and some pretty secure metal gates. Although it had no air conditioning inside, there was plenty of scope to have some installed, and the rent was less than 4,000 Thai Baht per month – around £75 at today's exchange rates.

Jum fell in love with the house, and we'd moved in by

end of the following day, thanks to a little cash gift here and there.

The next day we heard through the grapevine that Yai Dee had moved back into her home and Bitch #2 had resold our home for almost twice the amount she had paid us. This was standard behaviour for that gold digging little mare, and apparently both Yai Dee and her girlfriend had been spotted living it up on a pair of brand new scooters. It wasn't beyond the realms of possibility that the whole debacle had been arranged; I shuddered to think how badly it may have ended.

Tom was due to start KPS School in a few weeks, and I needed to get a bloody job. Our bank balance hadn't had an injection since the house sale, so it was time for me to try and remedy the situation. We'd had a good few weeks, nobody had been stabbed, and even Mum sounded a little more chipper when I called her. She had no idea what had happened to the package she was supposed to send, including my poor wedding ring, but I had resigned myself to never seeing it again. We'd managed to rent this house without Jum having an ID card, but pretty soon we would have to get this problem sorted.

But tonight, I needed to sleep. Tomorrow was another day.

.

The People's Democratic Republic of Laos

ME AND TOM IN LAOS

Chapter 11

Teaching

On a typically boiling hot day in Kalasin, Jum and I had literally walked from school to school with my CV. Even though this was 2011, emails and even phone calls were not the way that schools really functioned. It was all done on a face-to-face basis, and if that face didn't fit, you knew where the door was.

Even walking on the pavements was a challenge; if they weren't full of life-threatening potholes they were jam-packed with whatever the shops were selling. I had dressed conservatively in a polo shirt and a pair of cords, but within a few minutes the shirt was soaked with sweat and the cords were as comfortable as a pair of galoshes.

The first school we approached was Anuban Kalasin, a junior school of sorts with around 2,000 students. We waited in reception as the admin worker phoned our arrival through to the English department. After what seemed an age, I could hear footsteps approaching. A short, overweight black man announced his arrival in a booming voice.

'I am Elvis – and who are you?'

I knew immediately that this was not the school for me. But against my better judgement I followed him to another classroom and listened as Elvis and his wife told me about the school, explaining that I could actually work on a tourist visa despite the rules stating otherwise.

I knew for a fact that any teacher caught working in Thailand without a work permit and a Non-Immigration Type B visa would be detained and deported from the Kingdom of Thailand.

'Oh no, that simply is not the truth!' they both chorused, and we were joined by an attractive Thai lady who introduced herself as the head of English. Her spoken English was pretty good and as we all walked towards the main building, she explained that I needed to meet the school Director.

'So he can see how handsome you are,' she squealed with delight.

I was not so convinced, but followed, regardless.

Elvis knocked on the door and opened it almost immediately. We entered a huge office with a table that must have been at least 3 metres long. Sat at the other end was a man in his sixties, dressed to the nines in a white military suit complete with medallions and gold coloured pips on the shoulders, and totally involved in his food.

He was Thailand's answer to Idi Amin!

'Elvis! What do you want?' he bellowed in our direction.

'Mr Director Sir, I would like you to meet Mr Philip,' Elvis replied.

The Director gave me a sneer and returned to his chicken-foot salad.

'Philip is from the Ukraine.' Mrs Elvis had clearly been confused when I told her I hailed from the UK, and I almost forgave her, but when she explained that my OU degree was from an internet University, that was the straw that broke this TEFL teacher's back.

I was about to say a few choice words but Jum, reading my mind, squeezed my hand and whispered, 'Mai Poot… okay?'

She was asking me not to speak, knowing that in the past my ribald comments had usually made matters worse. We left the Director to his own devices, and before they could add insult to injury we made our excuse and fled the scene.

The rest of the day had been just as fruitless, and I was beginning to doubt that I'd ever teach – at least not here in Kalasin.

So how did I get the job in Kalasin Pittayasan School?

Just by a chance meeting a few days later at the market! I smiled to myself now as I recalled it. I was looking at some half-alive eels and was wondering about the cruel fate these poor buggers were about to meet, when I looked up and saw

Teaching

a well-dressed Thai lady giving me the once over. Just as I was about to move on to the next stall of tortured marine life, she asked me a direct question:

'Can you teach English?'

Thais were never slow in coming forward, and seldom wasted time on preamble or introductions.

'Well... I...'

'I think you look like an English man and maybe our school will give you a job.'

I smiled inwardly as I thought about Elvis and the other schools Jum and I had canvassed a few days earlier.

It turned out that Wannee was the Head of English at Kalasin Pittayasan School, the same school where Tom would be starting at in a few weeks' time.

I hadn't been there when Jum and Tom visited the school, and when Jum had asked if there were any teaching jobs going, she was told that all places were filled. It turned out that my soon-to-be predecessor had been signed up for another year at the school, but had fallen foul of one of the unwritten rules of Thai Education:

Students are not allowed to fail.

I struggled to get my head around the logic of that particular rule, but was still pleased that he had stuck with his guns and subsequently created this void for yours truly to fill.

Wannee told me to come to the school on Monday morning and to make sure I was dressed smartly, indicating that my current attire of shorts and flip flops would not really cut it. I rushed home to share my good news with Jum, and she looked immensely relieved. If I hadn't been able to find a job, I suppose we would all have been returning to the UK complete with tails between legs, and nowhere to go.

Of course, Mum would have let us stay with her and Dad in Fort William but that really did not appeal to me after our last visit. Dad's Vascular Dementia was getting worse, and every time I spoke to Mum I could hear the strain in her voice. She'd accepted some help in the form of several carers, who came in two's four times a day. I know that Mum hated any outside interference, no matter how well

Bangkok to Ben Nevis Backwards!

meaning it may have been.

Mum had been a teacher all of her life, so I decided to call her and break the good news. The phone rang for what seemed like an age before the answering machine kicked in. I left a brief message, wondering what she could be doing at this time of day.

It wouldn't be until a year or so later that I would learn the answer to that question.

So Monday morning came and Jum insisted on holding my hand for the whole event. We scootered our way to school – it was only one kilometre, if that, and although the new term hadn't started students seemed to be everywhere. The Language Department was on the first floor and as we made our way up the stairs, it began to sink in just what a huge school this was. KPS was a government institution, and had been around for over a hundred years. More than 5,000 students attended, with around 300 teachers; of these only seven or eight were foreigners like me.

Just as we were about the open the door, it was flung open and a tall black fellow welcomed us in.

'You are a very handsome man!' he exclaimed, and stuck out a huge hand for me to shake.

I squeezed just hard enough to show that I was no pushover, and he returned the favour. Introductions were made and I looked around the room, to see about forty pairs of semi-interested eyes giving Jum and I the once over. Wannee was not there, but we were shown some chairs and asked to wait. The lack of professionalism surprised me as I noticed the ramshackle tables and chairs, and it looked as if the whole room full of teachers, all female, were having a good old gossip – about us.

I felt a tap on my shoulder and turned to see a slim Thai lady of about thirty, smiling at me.

'Can you help me?' she said in a sing-song voice. This phrase was soon to be one of the most common I would hear in this particular room.

'Sure, no problem.' I smiled.

She skipped back to her desk and returned with a hefty book and some paper. This was the first time I met Pai, a Thai English teacher who had found an easy way to get her assignments completed for her Master's Degree. So I

Teaching

was the next victim. I grimaced inwardly as she explained the question and looked hopefully at me for some sign of acceptance. She needed a 500-word summary based on a chapter in the aforementioned tome, which resembled War and Peace. I wondered if this was part of the interview, and gave it my best shot.

Meanwhile Jum had wandered off to explore around the school. After all, her son and husband would soon be spending a lot of time here.

I only took twenty minutes to finish the mini-essay, and by the time I had handed it back to a beaming Pai, Wannee had arrived.

The interview was quite unlike anything I had ever experienced. It went something like this:
'How much salary do you want?'
'How much can you pay me?'
'What is Open University? I never heard of this!'
'It is a very fine British University.'
'Okay, can you start in two weeks?'
'Sure.'
'Your salary is 25,000 baht per month.'
'Um... okay.'
And that was that. I left to find Jum and we went out to celebrate my first ever teaching job.

So the morning of all mornings finally arrived and it was time for me to become a teacher; a giver of knowledge, a mentor; all of these things. Who was I trying to kid? My old buddy, self-doubt was already creeping in as I looked at my choice of attire for this massive day, and I wasted at least fifteen minutes simply looking at shirt-and-trouser combinations.

It was about 7 a.m. and the temperature was already hitting 30 degrees Celsius. I decided on black slacks and a white short-sleeved shirt. Jum had chosen these for me a few days earlier; we had bought them in the local Tesco supermarket.

Despite sharing the name and parent company with the consumer goods giant in the UK, the Thai version of Tesco was a far more adventurous place to visit and had a veritable treasure trove of oddities stacked in each aisle.

Bangkok to Ben Nevis Backwards!

It was when I was trying on the shirts and trousers in the changing rooms that I discovered I was carrying a little extra timber. I was always a short, stocky guy, but to discover my waist was now approaching 40 inches was a surprise.

When Jum had asked the shop assistant if she stocked any larger sizes, she'd cast me a slightly sympathetic look and scuttled off to the store room. Emerging ten minutes later with an armful of garments, she explained to Jum that these were the only shirts and trousers that would fit me. She referred to me as 'Khon Uan' (literal translation – 'Fat Person'). Thai people were often this frank and I had long since stopped being offended; what was the point?

I had, at first, been wont to fire off similar back-handed compliments to the 'offenders'. Years ago I was in the immigration office applying for an extension to my Tourist Visa. After handing in my documents, I was waiting for what seemed like hours to be called back to the officer's desk, and then I heard my name being bandied about.

'Hua Lan Yoo Sai?'

I was being referred to as 'baldy'! (This was entirely accurate of course.) To make matters worse, the offending gent was in possession of the world's most obvious wig. I was called back to the desk and, after a brief conversation, I smiled at the Elton John look-alike and asked him where I too could buy such a magnificent beast as that which currently adorned his bonce. Of course he didn't understand a word, so a helpful Thai lady who worked alongside him was only too happy to oblige. When the message eventually got through, his face turned a nasty shade of purple and I tried not to smile as he adjusted the toupee slightly.

But the last laugh was on me, because when he handed the passport back the letters 'REFUSED' were staring right back at me in bright red print.

Lesson learnt the hard way. From then on I always let similar remarks ride, just in case.

Anyway, back to the first day of teaching, and after deciding that I looked okay in the Tesco outfit, I went into Tom's room to wake him up. He was already developing into a handsome young man, with probably more European looks than Thai, and this type of feature went a long way in a country that was a little shallow when it came to judging

Teaching

one's personality over appearance. I'd been that age once, and remember how, all of a sudden, the opposite sex had started to become visible.

Checking myself out in his mirror and realising that a short, bald, overweight, middle-aged man was looking back at me, I wondered how the teachers and students would judge me...

Tom rolled over and reminded me that he wasn't due to start until tomorrow; I was on my own here.

Jum wished me luck and kissed me goodbye as I hopped on the bright yellow scooter and made my way to my new job. It was a beautiful day, and the light breeze against my face was most welcome as I sped my way to the school. It really seemed as if this was going to be a most excellent day. After all, I had spent seven years of study getting my Open University Bachelor's Degree and TEFL certificate. It would have been a crying shame if these pieces of paper had been nothing more than a little window dressing for a shop that was devoid of any real achievement or aspirations.

So a teacher I finally was, and as I pulled up outside Kalasin Pittayasan School and looked through the locked gates, I thought about the chain of events that had led to my employment at this huge establishment.–As I walked up the path towards the Language Department I winced; my foot had started to ache. I was prone to getting ingrown toenails and my latest one was a real beauty. The big toe on my right foot was going ballistic, as the nail had eaten into the side without mercy. Wearing formal shoes hade made matters worse, and I cursed myself for not getting this treated earlier.

I noticed some attention from the students, who were looking at me like a lion sizing up a young calf.

As I climbed the stairs and entered the Language Department I felt a chilled blast of air conditioning wash over me – most welcome. I looked around the room for a familiar face, but there were none. Nobody had even stood up to introduce themselves, so I looked around again and noticed a desk in the corner of the room with a name tag that read 'Phillip'. My name was spelt incorrectly, but I didn't really care. I walked over and tried to get comfortable in the small wooden chair. By now the toe was really hurting, and I was feeling a lightheaded.

Bangkok to Ben Nevis Backwards!

For we teachers, the first day was all about finding out who you were teaching, and preparing lesson plans. Gradually the room filled up and it soon became apparent that I was the only English, or rather Scottish, one here. Mustafa greeted me with a bone-crushing handshake and explained that he would be helping to make me feel comfortable on my first day. I had liked him from the offset; this larger than life character had a very friendly way about him.

The rest of the day was spent with me trying to get a first lesson plan together, and having a look around this massive school. Over 100 classrooms, some of them in buildings more than four stories high, no air conditioning and jam packed with chairs. I was gobsmacked to learn that there were up to 60 kids in a single class! How the hell would I manage?

Mustafa smiled and laughed like only he could as he let me in on a little trade secret: 'The students are lazy; they do not wish to learn from us. You need to entertain them, not teach them.'

Well, this guy had survived one year already so I suppose that he must have had a point.

I was studying my lesson schedule and was shocked to learn that some days I would be teaching for five hours in a row while on others, for only two lessons in the whole day. It seemed that English Conversation was not a priority, and whilst I would teach each of my 18 classes once per week, they would get three times as many lessons from their Thai English teacher!

Little wonder that the Thai students had such a poor grasp of spoken English; they were spending too much time wrestling with grammar and writing essays that they couldn't even read.

That evening I prepared myself for the first day proper, and was amazed to see that Tom wasn't in the slightest bit nervous. In fact, he looked as if it would be just another day. I kind of envied him as I wondered how the next twenty four hours would pan out.

My toe looked as if it was going to explode, swollen to the nines and frankly, starting to reek. Tomorrow was Thursday, so if I could last till the weekend I'd ask Jum to come with me to Kalasin hospital to have the nail removed.

Teaching

KPS SPORTS DAY

'Phil, is 25,000 baht per month enough for us to live on?'
The question came right out of the blue, but to be honest, I suppose I had been waiting for it to materialise.

I sat down with Jum and started to draw up one of my famous budgets.

Oh, I was quite the dab hand at getting it all down on paper, of that there was little doubt. However, when it came to manning up and following through, let's just say that I was an 'epic fail', as my son was so fond of saying these days.

My track record with money management spoke for itself – just a few steps away from bankruptcy only last year, so yes, Jum's query certainly needed to be given some thought.

In terms of straightforward maths, my plan went a little like this:

Bangkok to Ben Nevis Backwards!

Income:	+25,000 per month
Outgoings:	
Rent –	-4,000 per month
Food –	-4000 per month
Gas for the bikes –	-500 per month
All bills for house –	-3000 per month
Phones –	-700 per month

This left a whopping 12,800 baht!

Okay, that only worked out to be around £250 in real money, but living in Thailand was certainly cheap... or so I thought!

There was no stress in terms of debts, or worrying if the mortgage rates would rise – and when you consider that the typical Thai household of four managed to survive on 10,000 baht per month, we were quids in. We also had some money left from the house sale, although that was decreasing every day.

I planned to set up evening and weekend teaching classes once I found my way at the school, and perhaps Jum would also get a job. She was still using her British passport, thanks to the skulduggery performed by her lovely family. I still could not believe that this lovely woman was still in touch with those people! Considering what they had done to her, and us, in the last few years , I really believed that Jum should be next in line for the Nobel Peace Prize, or at least get a wooden spoon for 'Best Efforts'.

Not a day went passed when I watched her trying to deal with that hideous injury that resulted from the attack from Yai Dee. A broken arm and God knows how many pins in her elbow, plus the scar that made all other scars look like scratches. To make matters worse, the entire family had turned their backs on us and refused to co-operate with the police. Then, just a few months later, they all returned with hands outstretched as usual, looking as if butter wouldn't melt!

I had forgiven this bunch of misfits one time too many and still harboured evil thoughts of revenge as far as Yai Dee was concerned. About five years earlier, when she had fallen out with her younger sister, Hoi, the family had removed Jum's name from the house and, as described

Teaching

earlier, she was now unable to apply for an ID card – and without that, a Thai Passport couldn't be applied for.

Potentially this meant that it would be almost impossible for Jum to work in Thailand, yet the Clampetts still thought they could drop by for the occasional loan, even though their own actions had reduced our income!

I spent a good few minutes in hate mode, then looked up to see Jum had ironed my white shirt and was already preparing some Laos food to take to her oh-so-lovely mother the next day.

My damned toenail was starting to howl once more and I was thinking about taking the next few days of to get it seen to. In hindsight this would have been a very slick move, but I decided to tough it out... big mistake!

I said goodnight to Tom and crashed out early for the day.

Our new home had a decent garden but the damned thing was full of ants, snakes and frogs. It had rained heavily a few days earlier, so parts of the ground were wet, and even submerged, thanks to the huge wall that gave our home a compound-like feel.

This evening I had noticed a weird noise coming from one particular corner of the garden and as the light disappeared, a chorus started up. There were three distinct sounds:

Uuung Aanng
Reet reet!
Eeek eeek!

Each of these would be produced at different intervals, and when they coincided the cacophony was immense. Tonight of all nights it seemed to be the World Cup finals of the Kalasin Frog Ensemble, and although I was generally fascinated by nature, I really could have done without it on this particular night in May.

After an hour, Jum came to bed and was pretty much asleep not long after her head made contact with the pillow. I lay awake for what felt like days, and when I checked the time on my phone, it was almost 2 a.m.! I had to be in school in less than six hours, and the amphibious beasts

Bangkok to Ben Nevis Backwards!

were only just getting into their stride.

Then I heard a new sound, an extremely high pitched one at least three octaves above the rest. Whilst the original chorus backed off a little, this new combination was simply too much for me to bear.

As I sat upright and started cursing, Jum opened her eyes and said one word: 'Snake.'

She immediately dozed off again and I started to realise what she had meant. A snake must also have had enough of the out-of-tune slimy buggers, and was taking immediate action. But it wasn't the serpent making this din, it was his or her poor victim!

By now it was almost 2.30 a.m. and as I pulled on my slippers and mustered up the energy to join the party, Jum rolled over and said quite clearly, 'Be careful of Snake.'

I'd grown up with snakes in South Africa, where I had even caught cobras on occasion, improvising with swimming goggles to avoid the venom that spitting cobras like to spray at humans. But I was only 12 years old back then, and a lot faster than this 45-year old body could possibly manage.

As I pulled back the screen door I noticed all sounds seemed to have momentarily ceased, other than the screaming noise. This made it easier to track down, and I soon worked out where the murder was taking place. In the left hand corner of the compound, underneath the branches of our large mango tree, the water was deeper than anywhere else in the garden.

I used the flashlight on my mobile phone and picked up a large stick as I approached the hideous noise. As I neared, I could see a thrashing shape, and about ten feet short of the commotion I stopped for a closer look.

Although the phone's flashlight was just a single LED bulb, I knew I was within spitting distance of a Very Large Snake.

My knowledge of reptiles was actually pretty comprehensive, and judging by the size of this specimen, it was most probably some kind of python. Other than a few such as the Mamba and King Cobra, most poisonous snakes do not grow longer than 6 or 7 feet. This big boy was at least 10 feet in length and had some impressive girth action going on.

Teaching

My heart leaped a little, because after all, didn't I bring my family to Asia for some adventure and unpredictable events? Well, here was my first real slice of nature's finest having at it, right here in my garden!

I took a few more steps and must have disturbed the snake's meal time, because he appeared to drop the remains of the plump frog and turned to look directly at me.

His head and body almost immediately disappeared under the water, and I instinctively took a step back. By now, there were absolutely no sounds in the garden and it was as if only the snake and I were there, in a weird parallel universe.

For what seemed like an eternity, there was no movement, and I wondered if the serpent had simply decided to lay low until this rather tubby white human ambled off to bed. There was little chance of me doing that, because I knew that whatever this snake was, it was big enough to do some serious damage to my family – and could probably eat dear Megan whole.

Then I started to notice some ripples appearing on the surface. I took another step back as I realised the snake was coming in my direction.

'Phil, are you okay?' Jum's voice broke my concentration and I turned to see her face pressed against the screen window in our room.

'There is a big snake here and I need to do something about it!'

Within seconds she was by my side with an industrial-sized torch and a massive rake. 'Phil, it dangerous, come back inside!'

I wondered why she was saying this, as it was clear she had brought the correct tools for the job in hand. Then I heard a familiar noise as Megan came running towards us, barking like a bloody Jack Russell. She must have seen the snake before us, because she stopped a good ten feet short of where Jum and I were.

I turned back – and found myself looking at the largest King Cobra I had even seen, staring right back at me, eye to eye. It must have stood at least 5 feet off the ground, making its full length around 11 or 12 feet – a monster!

I loved snakes but immediately understood that there was no way I could catch this magnificent beast without

135

killing it – or it killing me. Christ, all I had wanted tonight was to get some semblance of sleep before the morning, and now I was reliving an episode of Steve Irwin's life, God rest his soul, in my garden!

Jum had disappeared, and so had Megan, but in an instant my dauntless wife was back – and this time had a different tool in her hands. She had ditched the rake in favour of one of the machetes with an elongated handle. Apparently these were used for cutting down sugar cane and bamboo, and were pretty good farming tools – amongst other things.

Before I could even think out my latest plan of action, the tiny woman next to me simply took four steps forward and let rip with the sugarcane machete, with all of her might. I gasped out loud as the hooded cobra seemed to break in two, leaping into the air as the audible thud of the machete hitting the soggy ground resonated in my ears. That poor beast was going nowhere.

Jum took my hand and as we walked back to the house she said two words:

'Go Sleep.'

A few minutes later I was just about to enter the land of nod when the frog chorus resumed, this time even louder than before. I imagined them speaking in tongues about the floorshow that they had just witnessed. One particularly large specimen was saying:

'Hah, did you see the slap-headed foreigner almost wet himself as his little wife killed that bastard snake?'

I smiled as I realised I must now be dreaming, because how could frogs tell Europeans from Thai people?

daylight came all too soon and as I dressed for the big day, I wondered about the snake and frogs and was it all a dream? Looking out of the window I saw the shape of the cobra's rather deflated head in the corner of the garden with about a dozen birds having their breakfast on the lawn. Although still an impressive size, in the light of day the snake wasn't quite the giant that my wife had done battle with last night. Strange that...

I felt sad because I hate the killing of any animal, but I also knew that a dead dog – or even a dead human – was a far higher price to pay.

Teaching

My phone told me that it was 7 a.m. and I had one hour before my first proper teaching day kicked off. I started to think about Mum and Dad and wished that they could be here, if even just for a week or two. But that would never happen...

As I put the little phone on the kitchen table, it spluttered into life and I could see three letters displayed on the screen: **MUM**

I felt excited because this was the first time she had called me in the six months we had been overseas.

'Hello Dear.' The familiar voice sounded in good form.

'Mum, it's great to hear from you! How are things?'

'We're okay, we are managing just fine.' Her reply was textbook Christina Hall; she was never one to complain. 'Listen Phil, I just wanted to call to say good luck today.'

She must have read my email; I was pleasantly surprised because I'd long given up on any kind of two-way conversation with Mum as far as the World Wide Web was concerned.

'Thanks, Mum!' I was stoked because this meant the world to me, I wanted her to be proud, and I guess I needed some kind of pep talk before the teaching gig really kicked off.

I then went into a bit of a diatribe about the previous night, the snake, the frogs, even the bloody dream. I was rambling because of excitement, nerves, and a little bit of fear I suppose.

'Oh dear, still playing with snakes after all these years, bless you!'

I started to explain that this was actually a little more serious, but she went on to say: 'I will always be proud of you Phil, and you really can do anything that you want to, I'v always known that.'

I was about to reply and ask about Dad, but the line went dead.

I tried calling back at least a dozen times but there was not even a network signal. It was now about 07h30 and I had to get a wriggle on to make it on time. Tom was due to start about half an hour after me but he took a lot longer to get going, especially after nearly six months out of the education system.

I kissed Jum goodbye and hopped on the little yellow scooter, all suited and booted for my first day of teaching.

Bangkok to Ben Nevis Backwards!

My toe was still giving me gyp, but the adrenaline of the whole occasion dampened that sensation.

As I drove down the main Kalasin Road towards the school I was aware of hundreds of school kids heading in the same direction. I wondered which ones I would be teaching, and before I knew it, I had reached my destination.

As I parked up the bike, the school grounds were already teeming with student life and I felt as though the school had been transformed into a mini city. With over 5,000 kids and 300 teachers, KPS was larger than some villages in the UK, and I started to think about the magnitude of my own role in this educational metropolis.

I made my way to the Language department and as I tried the door, I was surprised to find it locked! It was about 7.50 a.m. and I supposed that whoever held the key was running a little late.

Just outside the room was a little bridge that connected this block to another, so I decided to walk across the structure to get a better view of the whole place. The school was extremely impressive; each block had been painted in vivid colours, lending a real tropical feel to the establishment. As I looked directly towards the school gates I could see teachers arriving by car, scooter, and even bicycle.

The students were also pouring through the entrance. Some seemed to be carrying bags of fruit and what appeared to be a variety of street food in see-through packages. There is no way that the UK school would allow their students to bring hot snacks into the school, but Thailand had a very relaxed attitude towards food. In fact, the whole country seemed to be obsessed with eating – if you became hungry, everything else came crashing to a halt.

My line of sight was interrupted by a large flying insect, and I realised that I was actually stood directly below a hornets nest. I moved away and almost tripped; the floor surface of the bridge was very uneven. A few students who were watching me chuckled, and I felt a little embarrassed as I moved back to the Language Building.

By now it was almost 8 a.m. and the door was wide open. I was surprised to see at least six teachers already sat at their desks. I smiled and said good morning to them, and a few replied but most seemed less than impressed. As I made my way to my seat, I heard a few Thai words being

Teaching

bandied about which I recognised immediately:
'Hua Lan (bald).'
'Uan (fat).'
'Dtee-ah (short).'

I was waiting for the complete set but 'Na-Kleet (ugly)' didn't make it into the top three!

I felt a little annoyed, but also wasn't really surprised, and replied to nobody in particular in my best Thai:

'Wow, I have never worked with such beautiful ladies, have I walked into a modelling building by mistake?'

To say that the throng of female teachers were a little gobsmacked is an understatement. They looked at each other, then at me, and the red cheeks told me all I needed to know.

I got back to unpacking my bag and started to take a closer look at my schedule for the day. I had about three hours of free periods, and then a lesson before lunch. The afternoon was also fairly free, just a lesson right at the end. Each lesson was 50 minutes long, and on other days I was teaching some classes back-to-back for over four hours. I wondered about the heat and also whether my material would be up to scratch.

I was given two books, one for M3 and one for M4. They were a full year of lessons, and I had been told to use this as a source for my own classroom teaching plans. I was a little surprised to learn that I'd be writing and setting the exams for half-term and the end of term.

The most important thing to remember was that 'No Student Can Fail!' I use capitals because it was the reason why I had this job. As I said before, my predecessor had other ideas. He had failed several students, seeming to think that an attendance record of 20% was enough reason for this. Of course, he was asked to rethink his final score for these miscreants and whilst he retained the moral high ground, the school simply asked him to find other employment arrangements. He considerately did this, but only after he'd made the 2,000 mile round trip to extend his working visa. These visas are only good for one school, so the poor blighter would be making a repeat trip once he secured new employment.

This was the message that was hammered home from day one: 'Foreign Teachers must do as they are told!'

Bangkok to Ben Nevis Backwards!

Having spoken to other teachers over the last few months, mainly on the internet forums, I was under no illusion as to my new role. Less educator, more entertainer. Thai students get bored easily and many of them will never even need to speak English once they leave the bosom of KPS – even those who major in English in University will seldom need to converse in the language. I was soon to learn that most of the Thai English language teachers could hardly string a sentence together.

'Philip! Het Ngaan Yoo!'
My thoughts were disturbed by this loud salutation and I looked up to see the man-mountain Mustafa looking down on me, somewhat like an eagle about to consume a baby rabbit! I smiled back and he asked me, 'Do you understand what I have just said?'

I had an idea that he was using the Isaan dialect to ask what I was doing, or working on, but I replied in the negative, as I suspected he wanted to tell me anyway.

He said in his rather strong Ghanaian accent that he was speaking Laos/Isaan and asking what I was doing or working on.

'Wow, you can speak Isaan?' I said in fake astonishment.

'Yes! You too must learn this, because then the teachers and students will respect you!'

He strode off to his desk and I heard a few whispers from my group of 'admirers'. None of these seemed to be respectful though – quite the reverse.

In a few minutes Mustafa was back and told me in no uncertain terms that we must now go to the assembly area. I followed suit and as we made our way down the stairs I saw a familiar face. I was pleased to see Tom, surrounded by what appeared to be Thai female students all looking smitten by my handsome little boy.

'That boy is very lucky!' Mustafa told me in his booming voice. 'He will have many girlfriends because he is lookkrung!' (Half Thai, half European.)

I was about to tell him that Tom was my son, but he had already marched off towards what seemed like a sea of green jerseys. I could see at least 1,000 students moving in unison, and a few minutes later I saw the assembly area with another 4,000 sat in perfect lines as the Thai National

Teaching

Anthem crackled through a loud, but poor quality, PA system.

Mustafa was waiting for me, and as I was about to sit he reminded me that everybody had to stand during the Thai National Anthem. I took this opportunity to survey the scene, and the sight and sound of 5,000-plus students all signing in unison was very impressive.

As the track was faded out we sat down, and almost immediately another song began crackling through the speakers, one of which was directly above our heads. I smiled inwardly as I recognised the sounds of the Village People blasting through the school assembly area – *YMCA* being the song of choice!

A teacher on the stage was gesticulating furiously, and all the students began to imitate this track-suited lady as she initiated a very Butlins-esque dance routine. Mustafa was following suit, pulling me to my feet – this I was not expecting! It was already 35 degrees in the shade, and the last thing I really needed now was to be doing star jumps and the like.

But it seemed that all of the teachers were getting their own dance moves on, and I had to do the same. I tried to get away with as little as possible, and thankfully about four minutes later the punishment ended.

'Do you feel alive, my friend?' Mustafa was buzzing by now, and I was glugging away on the water bottle that Jum had insisted I brought with me to school.

'School is different in Thailand,' she had warned me, and I was beginning to see how different it really was.

After assembly we had a small snack by the coffee shop, and I was introduced to another foreign teacher. Her name was Bao, a pretty American lady in her mid-twenties.

She looked more than a little Thai, and she explained that she was actually born in North Eastern Thailand, to a hill tribe family. Sometime back in the 1980s, as a small child, Bao was airlifted to the U.S.A. as part of a United Nations programme, and had since become very American. She was back in Thailand to re-connect to her roots, and although she had asked the agency back in the States for a nursery role, preferably in either Bangkok or North-East Thailand, here she was in Kalasin.

Bao seemed less than happy about this fact, and was

also bemoaning the lack of any support from the school with regards her first ever teaching experience.

'They told me that I would have a Thai teacher to help me today, but that doesn't seem to be happening,' she grumbled.

Instead of teaching kindergarten kids, Bao would be teaching M2 and M4, 14-year olds and 16/17-year olds. I was teaching M3 and M4 Apparently M3 were always the toughest year to teach because the 16-year olds were full of hormones and really had little interest in learning anything, let alone English conversation.

We had a little huddle and promised to back each other up if necessary, and then I went back to my lesson plans as I started to think about my lesson at 11 a.m.

The schedule told me that I would be teaching M3/13. Apparently the /13 indicated a top tier class according to the Thai streaming system, and I was thinking about the best way to tackle this challenge. Wannee still hadn't appeared and, as for Bao, she had indicated that I would have some help for at least the first introductory lessons.

I decided to use a tried and trusted TEFL icebreaking exercise that involved each student coming to the front of the class and introducing themselves. I had already printed out hundreds of sheets of paper, each with about 20 sets of questions, ready to cut into little cards. Each one had the same set of 5 questions:

> What is your name?
> How old are you?
> Where do you live?
> Describe your family?
> What is your favourite band?

I figured that these would take around a minute to answer verbally, and with around 50 or 60 kids per class, plus my own introduction, that would take care of the first lesson.

I had about 25 minutes before my first-ever foray into teaching, so decided to take some fresh air out on the bridge. As I stopped well short of the hornets' nest and looked below me, the bridge started to shake and I felt as if the whole structure was going to collapse.

Teaching

'My friend, why are you not teaching?' It was the unmistakeable sound of Mustafa as he took a few steps to the left while passing the hornets.

I explained that my first lesson would kick off in about twenty minutes and he offered to come along with me for moral support. I was fairly sure that I knew where the classroom was, but according to Mustafa I had this totally wrong. Apparently, 3/13 was in another block and he would show me the way – just as soon as he had chatted up the pretty new American Teacher.

Bao was less than impressed as Mustafa tried in vain to get her to come along on a date later that day. She was having a time of it because her first lesson was also starting at 11:00 and she asked me to help her get through this fifty minutes of uncertainty.

I had to say no because mine was running in tandem. I did suggest that Mustafa could accompany her, but strangely she wasn't keen.

'Okay, Mr Philip, let us go and teach!' boomed Mustafa.

So we were off and I tried to keep up with the 6 foot 4 inch 20-something man-mountain as we crossed the assembly area to the furthest block in the school. We climbed the three sets of stairs and, according to Mustafa, 3/13 was the furthest classroom from the Language Department. Mustafa was already in the room before I reached the doorway to see that this was in fact – 5/13!

It was almost 11:00. Making his apologies, Mustafa broke into a little run and told me that he now remembered where the classroom really was. My ingrown toenail had decided to make an its presence known, and this time it meant business. Still we climbed more stairs, and crossed a bridge – only to find that this was in fact 6/13!

At this point it was well after 11:00 and I wondered if Mustafa was just playing games with me.

'Mustafa, I know where the bloody classroom is!'

'Why didn't you say?

I had said, but had bowed to his superior knowledge, since he had already been teaching here for a year. My bad.

Finally we reached 3/13. It was already 11:20.

When I walked into the class it appeared that the students had decided to give up on me, and were already halfway through what seemed like a biology lesson instead. One of them was playing the role of teacher and as I looked at the whiteboard, I could see a diagram of a man who appeared to have three legs.

On closer inspection the middle leg was – well, exactly that! Above his head the name 'Mustafa' was scrawled, and I chuckled inwardly because the Thai students' sense of humour didn't appear to be that far off the British equivalent.

I was about to introduce myself, but the big man was one step ahead.

'Students! Please sit down!' he boomed, and they begrudgingly did so.

'This is Teacher Philip!'

They looked towards me and seemed distinctly non-plussed. I couldn't blame them because my tardiness was hardly going to win them over. I told Mustafa that I would take it from here and he went off for a toilet break, promising to return in a few minutes.

MUSTAFA

I looked around the class and for the first time, the enormity of my new role hit home. These 16 year olds were

Teaching

all waiting for me to say or do something and I felt rather nervous and even a little shy. How pathetic was I? 45 years old, and with plenty of life experience and travelling under my belt, how could I feel this way in front of children who had most probably never left the country of their birth?

'Hello Students!' I prayed that my greeting would be reciprocated and was so happy when they all replied.

Then a voice at the back barked out, 'All stand up!'

And they did.

'Good Morning Teacher, how are you?'

I was on a roll here.

'I am fine students, how are you?'

'We are fine!'

'Please sit down.'

And they did.

Well, this was going far better than I had expected.

I told the class where I was from and then wrote my name on the whiteboard.

'Students, please can you write my name in your book?'

They all seemed to understand – after all, this was the top stream – and as they obeyed I started handing out the 5 questions. It wasn't easy because the desks were so close together, I had difficulty squeezing through the gaps. I then wrote the 5 questions on the board.

I was pleased that although Mustafa hadn't yet returned, within a few minutes the students were coming to the front, in twos, and were answering the questions.

I had originally calculated that this exercise would see me through, and listened with more than a little pride as they belted through their answers to the rest of the class.

'My name is Jackie, I am 16 years old, I was born in Kalasin, I have one sister and my favourite band is One Direction.'

I was a little surprised at the last declaration, as the group cited had come second in the UK X-factor just a year ago and I had no idea they'd become such a worldwide success already. Oh well.

As Mustafa returned to the room I realised that all of the students had completed the task in hand and were looking to me for further instructions. Looking at my watch I realised that there was still fifteen minutes left! I counted the number of students and, to my dismay, discovered that this class only had 30, and not the 50 or so I had calculated for!

Mustafa must have sensed my concern and offered to take over for a few minutes if I needed a toilet break. I was glad to accept, and as I washed my hands and face in the bathroom I looked in the mirror and noticed that I was sweating heavily.

I hadn't been prepared, and I heard Jum's voice as I remembered her words, 'Phil, I am not sure you can be a teacher. You don't even like kids!'

This may have been true, but I was having a good stab at the profession my mother and sister had chosen – surely I could last another 10 minutes without lesson plans?

The toenail thought otherwise and began to throb like billio.

I walked back into the class and was shocked to see Mustafa bouncing around on one foot singing what I recognised as 'Father Abraham'. Or was it 'Simple Simon'? Half of the class were attempting to copy him while the rest were filming this spectacle on their smartphones. No doubt Mustafa and his crazy dance would be trending around Isaan schools before lunchtime was over.

For a large man he was remarkably nimble, and by now the temperature in the class must have been in the mid-40s.

'Mustafa, can we carry on with the lesson?' I pleaded, as he took a huge leap backwards, and I suddenly felt the weight of a 17-stone man come crashing down on my ingrown toenail.

I must have passed out because when I awoke, I was on the floor slumped against the wall. I looked up to see at least 30 faces looking down on me, and yes, the smartphones were out in force. I could only wonder how much of the event had already been recorded. They wanted entertainment and, by God, had we delivered!

My toe was past agony, and as I got to my feet I looked at the time on my watch and realised I must have been out for at least five minutes. The students were already leaving the room for lunch and Mustafa was looking apologetic, if a little impish.

'I can't do this, teaching is not for me,' I stated firmly.

His face took on a concerned look and he tried his best to reassure me. 'The students like you; they think you are handsome and very funny!'

Teaching

This didn't have the desired affect and I knew that my toe was beyond any help I could give any longer – I needed to get to a hospital.

'Mustafa, please tell Wannee or whoever that I have to leave, I will be back in touch but have to go to the hospital.'

He nodded and we went our separate ways.

I negotiated my way towards where my bike was parked and as I crossed the little bridge I must have caught my bad foot on the railings, because all hell broke loose in the hornets' nest and at least three of the buggers came for me.

I tried to run but it was no use; I felt a sharp pain on my nose and recoiled as I realised one of them had stung me! The combined pain from this and my ingrown toenail were just too much to bear. I stumbled down the stairs straight past a smiling Wannee and towards my yellow scooter, unashamedly whimpering.

There at last, I plonked myself onto the red hot seat and turned the key.

Nothing.

I tried about five times more; by now was fuming. Words were coming out of my mouth that certainly were not part of my lesson plan.

'Kick, kick!'

I turned my head and saw an elderly Thai man who was dressed like a janitor, doing a great impression of somebody kick-starting a motorbike.

I thanked him, but there was no way my foot could take any more strain. In anguish I pushed the poor scooter to the ground before limping off towards the school gates.

'But Phil, what about your lessons?'

I could make out Wannee's voice and turned back to see at least 500 students, all grinning at me, and the unmistakable shape of Mustafa and his pearly whites beaming in my direction.

To hell with this! I turned and walked out of the school, and in my mind I would never set foot in the hideous place ever again.

I tried calling Jum but there was no answer, and the combination of the heat, the exploded toenail and the damned hornet sting had all but finished me off. A few fruit sellers broke away from their gossip about the price

Bangkok to Ben Nevis Backwards!

of Durian these days, gave me the once-over, and chuckled to themselves as I slumped on to the pavement outside the school. I watched helplessly as the last remains of the phone battery faded away. Sitting on the kerb outside Kalasin Pittayasan School, I shook my head and finally admitted defeat.

Chapter 15

ENTERTAINER OR EDUCATOR?

As the huge hypodermic needle pumped what seemed like gallons of anaesthetic into my toe, I looked around the room and could see all types of candidates for the latest 'Walking Dead' box set. On the narrow metal bed next to me lay a child who couldn't have been any more than three, with a massive head wound, screaming loud enough to wake the dead on a different continent. A couple who must have been his parents were comforting him, but even I could see that this poor mite needed medical attention immediately.

My ingrown toenail was hardly life threatening, and as I tried to explain to the doctor that maybe she should be looking at the boy instead of me, she wiggled the massive needle around just enough to send a shockwave of pain through my entire body. A bespectacled young doctor appeared. He swiftly pulled the curtain around the young patient, and I returned my gaze to my toe just as the weapons-grade nail cutters were produced.

Jum was busy chatting to the old lady on our left, and as the doctor sliced through my septic nail I did my level best to remain as calm as possible. Jum's new friend was watching intently as half of my nail was ripped out of my toe; then she looked at my face, waiting for me to start howling like a little girl.

She was disappointed, because I maintained my composure, and just as she was about to ask Jum how she had found such a tough foreigner for a husband my wife let the cat out of the bag and explained that I had about a pint of painkiller floating around my veins.

The rest of the procedure was fairly simple, and we were soon on our way back home. Because we were by then well into the monsoon season, the rain was relentless and due to the usual blocked drains, the roads were under about 10 inches of water. I had to tie a plastic bag over my poor foot in order to stop any infection, and this made our trip home a little more eventful than usual.

Once we got there I had to explain to Jum about why I hadn't been able to complete my first day of teaching, and before I could finish Wannee's car was at our gates.

Great! I'd just had a surgical procedure on my toe, almost drowned on my motorbike and now I had to face KPS's version of the Spanish Inquisition.

She listened patiently as I did my best to explain the events leading up to my hobbling exit from the school. Her porcelain features barely creased when I told her about the hornet sting, and how I felt like giving up teaching after such a disastrous day. Instead, she was more concerned about the brand of tea that Jum had served up, and they chatted away for a goodly time while I did my best to look as pitiful as possible.

'Phil, you will come back to school tomorrow?' Wannee asked me.

I thought about the alternatives, and although I wasn't feeling my best, the idea of failure didn't exactly appeal either. I answered in the affirmative and Wannee left, but only after getting directions to the grocery store where Jum had found that fantastic green tea.

In stark comparison, Tom came home a little later and regaled us with tales of his awesome first day at school. He had been quite popular back in the UK, but this experience was altogether different. It seemed that the girls wanted to be with him, and the boys wanted to *be* him. My son was as happy as I had ever seen him.

This made me feel a lot better about my day, and after an early dinner I retired to bed for the night. My dreams were particularly vivid; I can remember being chased around the school by a 20 foot tall Mustafa as I hopped pathetically around the staircases.

The raucous din made by our frogs rudely awoke me from my bizarre thoughts, and when I heard an all too

Entertainer or Educator?

familiar scream, I went back to sleep rather than repeating the previous nights' heroics.

My second day as an English teacher in KPS couldn't have been any more different. Despite offers from Wannee to hold my hand for my first few lessons, I went to each class alone – to my surprise, with some success.

There were two classes in the morning and two in the afternoon, adding up to around four hours of teaching. This meant that I had four hours of free time in which to prepare my lessons, plus a one hour lunch break. The whole week pretty much mirrored this pattern, and I noted that I was only teaching for 20 hours per week. The downside was that my students would only get one hour of English per week, and that was no way nearly enough.

I was forced to wear sandals for at least a week as my poor toe needed some pressure-relief in which to heal properly. As I limped into each classroom, the 50 or so kids would all notice my footwear and the large bandage on my toe. They'd wait for me to introduce myself and, once the pleasantries were dispensed with, they'd ask about my injury.

I replied 'Lep Kop' (Thai for ingrown toenail).

To my surprise, not a single student laughed or even smirked. 'Lep Kop', they would repeat, and I even got some looks of sympathy, which rather helped with the bonding period. I could only imagine the amount of stick I would have got if I was a new teacher back in the UK.

Although teaching in Thailand was never plain sailing, the respect that I got from the students made it a very memorable experience that I will never forget. By the end of the second day I was definitely enjoying my new profession, and this was reinforced even more by the end of the week.

Tom was doing well, and I must admit that I played up the fact that he was my son on occasion. The girls would ask me if I knew him, and when I explained that he was my child, they would start asking all kinds of questions and even begged me for his mobile phone number.

I was teaching Mathayom 3, commonly known as the most difficult year to teach. The kids were aged around 15-16, and we all know how this particular hormone-riddled bunch of teenagers usually play up.

Bangkok to Ben Nevis Backwards!

The classes were labelled 3/1 all the way up to 3/14. 3/13 and 3/14 were known as the Talented Students League, or TSL for short. 3/1 to 3/3 were good kids. 3/4 to 3/10 were kind of the middle stream, and as for 3/11 and 3/12... well, let's just say that these were the most challenging.

But for some reason, over the whole year, it was these kids that I got on with the best. Okay, some of them were probably borderline ADHD, and God knows I didn't have the tools to deal with this type of behaviour, but I did my best. I managed to mix up my lessons enough for them to retain some level of interest, and to this very day I miss those little monsters!

My own set of objectives was fairly plain:

- Teach Conversational English
- Make lessons fun
- Turn up for lessons

That was pretty much it, and when I sat in on some of the Thai English teachers' lessons, I discovered something that really surprised me. Almost none of them, especially among the older ones, could speak a word of intelligible English!

They were essentially teaching reading and writing, and their grammar was probably better than mine, but conversational English was not their forté. I was often consulted by them in the staff room to double-check their pronunciation, and this was not always easy. I did my best to correct them without making too big a deal about it, but on occasion I failed miserably.

After about one month of teaching I'd had such a good day that I decided to call Mum and share my thoughts with her. Mum had taught for the best part of 30 years, and I just had the urge to talk about my own triumphs so far. But when we connected her mind was clearly on other things, and I listened as she told me how badly Dad had deteriorated in the last few months.

Mum sounded really strained, and I learnt that her doctor had arranged for two carers to pop in twice a day to check on her and Dad. Mum had always been a private

Entertainer or Educator?

person, and it was clear that this intrusion wasn't exactly welcome.

I started to wonder again about what would happen next as far as Mum and Dad were concerned. It is very difficult to come to terms with your parents struggling with old age. In fact, nothing prepares you for this inevitable set of circumstances and I must confess that I was guilty of simply pushing the whole thing out of my mind at times.

I didn't even get the chance to tell Mum how well I had done, and after that particular phone call I felt as flat as Holland. Here I was, a middle-aged man who still needed the approval of his parents!

Chapter 13

Teaching in Thailand – My Opinion

I could easily write a whole book about my year at KPS, and Tom could probably write several, but instead I have picked the most memorable moments for this record, and for your entertainment.

An honourable profession?

I had looked forward to becoming a teacher for years and the thought had never crossed my mind that this particular job would be considered anything but decent and respectable.

How wrong I was.

I'd started to read a few ribald comments online about English teachers in Thailand and although I resisted the temptation to wade in, I found it somewhat frustrating. It was more than just a case of the old cliché that goes something like this: *Those who can, do; those who can't, teach...*

Amongst expats here in Thailand, the general consensus seems to be that most TEFL teachers are a mixture of alcoholics, misfits and paedophiles. In my year of teaching I saw a mixture of the first two but I couldn't say if I saw any of the third.

In KPS, I was the only Native English speaker apart from a nice American lady named Alison. They hired a Frenchman and several African teachers, and even a Filipina. I was also shocked to learn that in Thailand, they preferred Native English Speaking teachers are from the USA and Canada.

Bangkok to Ben Nevis Backwards!

When I explained to several older Thai English teachers in my best Queen's English that I was actually born in Scotland, they both looked so disappointed.

'So Philip, you are not a Native English Speaker then?' I tried in vain to explain that I was British but in the end I gave up.

There was a small shop near the bus station that sold cheap booze, and this was the place where the English teachers who liked a drop of the hard stuff would congregate most evenings. I was glad to avoid these guys, to be honest, and when I met a few of them and noticed the bleary eyes and whisky breath, I started to see where the bad reputation was coming from.

Okay, I was no saint, but I made damn sure that I never touched any alcohol on a school night.

Memorable Teachers

I have already mentioned Mustafa, and I'll add a little more about the big guy in a later chapter, but there were a few other notable characters that deserve to be discussed here for a variety of reasons:

Kosuke
This chap was a total gent, and in true Japanese style he was extremely polite, and never imposing. He did have a penchant for falling asleep however, and I suspected that he may have a case of Sleep Apnoea. For a very slight man, Kosuke could eat a huge amount of food.

He once came on a 4-day break to one of the islands with my family, and we shared a coach journey of about 10 hours. In that time I witnessed him put away enough food to knock out a horse, despite weighing less than 8 stone. Kosuke was often a guest in our house and he would cook up a storm with his fantastic Sapporo cuisine skills.

One day he offered to cook some true English food for us, and after arriving with a few bags of groceries, he locked himself into our kitchen for several hours. By the time he was ready to serve the Hall family was absolutely starving. We watched, somewhat gobsmacked, as he approached the dinner table with a grin as wide as his face would allow. The plate was piled high with what could only be described as

Teaching in Thailand – My Opinion

egg mayonnaise sandwiches! They were as perfect as could be, cut identically and immaculately presented, but – they were what they were! To this day we still miss this Japanese gentleman and hope to be reunited one day.

Wannee
The teacher who offered me the job in the first place, a true lady. A little headstrong at times. I'll speak a bit more later about her attempts to find love online, but overall I have a lot of time for Wannee, and she and Jum are friends to this day.

Kwan
My Boss, and a very nice guy, if a bit touchy-feely. Always smiling and although in charge of about 40 foreign teachers, never seemed to be stressed whatsoever. His wife was also a nice lady, but far more scary than Kwan!

Palmmy
One of the most friendly teachers in KPS, and always happy to lend a hand. I was saddened to learn that she died earlier this year, and my thoughts are with her husband and children.

Santa Claus and his little helpers

Although Thailand is a Buddhist country, it does celebrate Christmas, and KPS certainly enjoys this festival. Whilst they probably don't really get the religious side of it, they love Santa Claus and all the trimmings. Let's be honest, the UK and most of the Western world have long since forgotten about baby Jesus, and Christmas is simply an excuse for a holiday, a few drinks and some extravagant gifts.

There is no official holiday for Christmas in Thailand, and on the 24th December Kwan asked me a rather strange question: 'Philip, do you have a Santa Claus costume?'

I replied in the negative and off he went at an alarming pace towards the stock room. He returned a few minutes later with a bin bag that appeared to be full of tinsel and Christmas decorations. Rummaging through the contents, he looked like the proverbial Isaan Cheshire Cat when he produced a fairly sad looking Father Christmas outfit. But there it was: red trousers, jacket, hat and white beard!

On Christmas morning I was 'ordered' to don this costume and, with Tom dressed as one of my little helpers, we did a little dance on the stage in front of 5,000-plus students and then walked amongst the seated throng, distributing candies.

Not every kid got a sweet because 300 doesn't really go into 5,000, but we had a laugh and although I was totally drenched in sweat, thanks to the double layer of clothing and 40-degree heat, it was a Christmas day that myself and Tom will never forget. It was also one of those rare father-son moments that I will treasure forever.

XMAS DAY IN KPS

Stubborn Teacher

Whilst most of the Thai teachers were pleasant enough, there were one or two who were clearly less than impressed with the foreign contingent. True to form, I managed to bump heads with one of these fine fellows.

Many of the classes that I taught involved me travelling

Teaching in Thailand – My Opinion

to that particular form room, and most of the time it was devoid of teachers so I could simply stroll in, say hello and crack on with the lesson in hand.

This was the case with 3/6, with whom, despite their being a rowdy bunch of kids, I had some kind of connection. The door was usually open and they could see me approaching as I left the stairwell on the second floor, and ambled towards them.

But one day the door was closed and as I got closer I could hear a male Thai voice bellowing out instructions, so I decided to wait outside until this lesson ended.

Except it didn't end.

I was due to start teaching 3/6 at 15:00. By 15:10 the previous lesson was still in full flow.

At this point I decided to make my presence known with a loud knock on the door. The lesson continued and, if anything, his voice was even louder.

I waited five more minutes and knocked again, but this time I also opened the door and was met with a sea of rather fearful faces – as if warning me of my impending doom.

I walked in and smiled at the 50-something Thai teacher, who was a pretty big guy. He sneered at me and returned to the whiteboard. Feeling rather non-plussed I retreated and waited politely outside.

Eventually he packed up and left, but as he walked passed me there wasn't an ounce of recognition, let alone an apology. I re-entered the room and could sense the relief on the faces of my poor students. I looked at my watch and realised that this oaf had stolen a good half hour of my lesson; by the time I had explained today's task, the bloody thing was over.

The class explained to me that this teacher was considered to be a bully by all of the students, and even some of his peers. He also had little time for foreign teachers, especially middle-aged bald ones such as yours truly.

I spoke to Ajarn Kwan and Wannee about this problem and they both gave the same answer: 'This man is very stubborn Phil, and he doesn't like foreign teachers.' They offered little in the way of help. I was pretty much left to deal with this dilemma alone.

I was learning that Thai people do not like confrontation and will usually do what they can to avoid them. I had no issue with this, but was mindful that I couldn't go around upsetting other teachers; this was not my stamping ground. I was here to help, not to make enemies.

The next week it was a repeat performance, and I could sense that he was getting some small pleasure out of the whole thing. So I decided to do something about it.

I spoke to Ajarn Kwan and told him that I was thinking about helping the Thai teachers with their English. I would come 5 or 6 minutes early to my classes, and if the Thai teacher was happy with this arrangement, I would include them in my English lessons and hopefully they would get something positive from this experience.

He agreed, and by the end of the week Kwan had told all of the Thai teachers who taught directly before me that I was hoping to include them in my English lessons.

But another Thai trait is their absolute fear of losing face – teachers were especially known for this. I figured that if he held the English language in such disdain it probably stemmed from a fear of the unknown, and I guessed that he would definitely not want to appear to know less than the very students he'd been berating just a few minutes earlier.

My plan had an amazing effect, because the next time I went to teach 3/6, the big man was nowhere to be seen. In fact, I never saw him in the classroom again. I'd had a minor win, and was really pleased that it hadn't resorted to a more basic ending.

The only downside was that about seven of the teachers were more than happy to be included in my lessons, and this created a lot more work on my behalf.

You win some, you lose more.

The Punisher

Although corporal punishment in schools was abolished from the UK back in 1999, I saw plenty of evidence of it at KPS, despite an apparent outlawing that was put in place in 2005.

I'd had plenty of experience being caned when I went to school in both the UK and South Africa, and it wasn't a pleasant memory. I first noticed it rearing its ugly head in KPS one day when I was at morning assembly.

I saw a surly-looking teacher walking amidst the seated

students with a sour look on his face. Behind his back was a thin stick about 2 feet long and less than half an inch wide. I was just wondering what the purpose of this was when my questions were answered.

He grabbed a small boy by his collar and let rip with the weapon. In less than a few seconds he had hit the boy more than half a dozen times, dropped him back on the floor and was back on the hunt.

It appeared to have the desired effect for at least a few minutes, while he spotted his next prey and dispatched them in a similar fashion.

There wasn't much that I could do so, I tried my best to ignore this barbaric behaviour.

That was, until the Punisher stepped over the line.

My son Tom was asked to read some English in front of the school in morning assembly. As he took to the stage, I noticed that he didn't look as smart as usual. In fact, his shirt hadn't been ironed and his belt was missing. This hadn't gone unnoticed. Pretty soon the Punisher was circling, with an evil glint in his eye.

As my son left the stage, I made my way before him and was just in time to prevent a nasty scene. The Punisher had already lifted his striking arm and was just about to let rip when I stepped between him and Tom.

He stopped, but if looks could kill, well – I would either be looking down on KPS at that moment from a very great height, or staring up from a place even warmer than Kalasin in March.

The head teacher came over and I explained that as a father, I couldn't let the Punisher do this. In fact, I explained that corporal punishment was now illegal and advised both parties to bear this in mind before making their next move.

Let's just say that I made an enemy that day and for once, it was for the *right* reasons.

KPS Got Talent

Did I mention that Thai students get bored easily and need entertaining? This was proven to me very quickly, and I decided to come up with a plan to keep them interested whilst also learning a little more about Western culture.

I was teaching 18 classes in total and each class had

Bangkok to Ben Nevis Backwards!

roughly 55 students, so when I was faced with nearly 1,000 bored faces in a single week, I started talking about something that I just knew would pique their interest: music!

In particular, the music from the UK and USA.

In the beginning I asked each class to split into groups of 4 or 5 people, and gave them their remit:

1. Find 3 or 4 friends to form a band with
2. Choose a name
3. Design a logo
4. Choose a song
5. Practice the song
6. Perform the song

It sounded simple enough, but pretty soon the whole school was talking about *KPS got Talent,* and I seemed to have created a monster.

I asked the director whether the school could donate something to the winning band, and also if we could stage a live show for the top ten bands. I got a firm negative for both requests, and despite the huge interest that my competition was generating I was starting to sense some resentment.

I was to learn that foreign teachers were not really supposed to do anything other than turn up for lessons and do what they were told.

This wasn't really me.

KPS got Talent was soon taking over M3 and M4, and I was loving it! The kids were learning English from a different source to the usual twenty year old workbooks, and this was both fresh and motivational.

It lasted for a good two months, and some of the talent was truly breath-taking. Eventually I had ten finalists, and had even created a Facebook page that featured about 20 videos. This was only visible to the KPS students, and had about 3,000 likes.

I planned to stage an event for the *gran finale* but sadly, it was never to be. It seemed that each band that had made the finals started to show signs of disinterest, and one by one they all pulled out of the show. It was only months later that I found out they had been told by a few teachers that if they took part in the show, there would be consequences.

The sad thing is that at least three of these groups were

Teaching in Thailand – My Opinion

then entered into external school talent shows, unbeknownst to me at the time. The respective Thai teachers took all the glory –a bitter pill for me to swallow.

On a good note, I managed to find a winner by way of hosted videos on a closed Facebook page; the band with the most 'Likes' was eventually crowned the KPS champs. I donated my electric guitar, amplifier and some cash to the winners – Three Direction!

KPS GOT TALENT – WINNERS

Testing?

After a few weeks into the first term, I was told about the mid-term tests and was surprised to learn that I had the responsibility of setting the questions! The results would count towards the overall grade for the year, and I'd also be asked to design the end of term tests as well as the exams for the 2nd term.

Considering I had nearly 1,000 students to test and subsequently mark, this was a serious amount of work, and no small responsibility.

I decided to mix the tests up and included verbal

Bangkok to Ben Nevis Backwards!

challenges as well as written and reading exercises. The mid-term tests took about two weeks, and almost as long again to mark them. Basically, my two week break was spent marking the results, but I didn't mind because I kind of enjoyed seeing how the respective classes had performed. I'd also had fun watching them take the tests, and walked from class to class as they worked through the questions with plenty of head scratching in evidence.

When I returned to KPS after the two week 'break' I was armed with eighteen sets of classroom report cards, and then spent another week entering these into the somewhat antiquated KPS spreadsheet system.

It was only after I had sweated blood and tears over the whole process that I noticed Thierry, my French colleague, had spent very little time with his own marking exploits. When I asked him how his kids had done, he smiled at me and replied, 'Phil, it don't really matter, they all pass...'

When I asked him what he was talking about, he reminded me that no Thai student at a government school can be allowed to fail. Failure makes the school look bad, and the teacher is always blamed. He'd simply binned the exam papers and given every one of his students a 3 or a 4. 3 was 75%, and 4 was the Full Monty. Thierry had spent less than three hours on his entire mid-term efforts, and the school were happy with his results.

Me? Well, I had failed about 10% of my students and was told in no uncertain terms that this simply was not good enough.

I took the report cards back home and returned them the next day. Kwan took a look at the cards and his eyebrows were raised so high that I thought they might leave his head altogether.

'Philip, all of your students have scored maximum for their tests!'

I wasn't sure if this was a question or simply rhetorical. 'Yes Ajarn Kwan, they are very good students, very good indeed.'

He looked up and without a hint of sarcasm replied: 'Philip, you are a very good teacher.'

Thierry smiled and winked at me as he told me: 'You are learning, boy, you are learning.'

His smile was short-lived however, because just as we

were about to leave for lunch together, Kwan called Thierry back and scolded him for not teaching his students as well as I had...

Another small win!

Taking your kid out of UK education – good or bad?

One of the questions that has been asked many times since coming back to the UK was: 'How could you take your child out of the UK schooling system?' This was usually accompanied with some kind of frown, and no matter what my answer happened to be, they had already labelled me as an unfit parent.

I suppose if I was only worried about Tom's schooling and nothing else, we'd never have left the UK. Of course I knew that his education was very important, but so was his personal development. Over the 18 months that we spent away from the UK, I watched as my 13-year old son turned into a young man who grew in both stature and confidence.

Was this a direct result of his travelling and cross-cultural experiences? I really do think so. In fact when we returned to Wallingford after six months or so in Scotland and the Asian escapade, Tom was derided by a few kids who told him in no uncertain terms that he would not only be behind, but also would probably not even get through the 6th form.

Surprise surprise... about a week before I wrote this piece, two of these 'friends' were asked to leave 6th form because they had failed all of their A level courses just one year in.

Tom? He's doing great, and on course to get distinctions.
I rest my case, M'Lud...

Chapter 14

THE MAN FROM DELTA FORCE AND OTHER INDISCRETIONS

Although we spent a good deal of the total 18 months in Thailand, this book isn't just about those experiences. I have also tried to capture my thoughts about how we as a family have coped when trying to start a new life, when the loved ones we leave behind are very much alive and not even remotely a closed chapter.

How do you manage when as you are finally embarking on a new episode in your life, you realise that the very people who brought you into the world suddenly need your help? And that if that help isn't forthcoming, you will become somehow directly connected to circumstances that could lead to their demise?

Do you stay – or do you go?

There isn't a stock answer that fits this dilemma because sometimes, you are so committed to your objectives that anything other than following through would be a total disaster. We did what we thought was right – but you will have to read the rest of the book to see how that panned out!

That being said, I've included a few more Thai-based happenings that are worth sharing, if only because they were such unique experiences that I thought they would add some value to the whole written journey.

Each of these encounters really happened, and whilst they may not be that amazing, I was constantly taken aback at the frequency with which they occurred. If anything, they added serious depth to the overall set of memories that the Hall Family will never forget.

Man from Delta Force

Our house was about one hundred yards from the main road, and we enjoyed the solitude that living on a quiet side lane brings. Opposite our front gate there was a large building which was being used as a kind of halfway-house for battered wives and the odd destitute soul.

One morning there was a knock on our door, and I opened it to find that one of the care workers had come over with a request. Although his English was probably better than most of the Thai English teachers in KPS, he seemed more comfortable talking to Jum.

To cut a long story short, he explained that a foreign man in his early sixties had been badly beaten up and was in Kalasin hospital. This poor chap seemed to have no money and wasn't exactly forthcoming as far as his name and circumstances were concerned. He wanted to know if Jum and I could possibly go to the hospital and ask him some questions. The shelter would be able to help him, but would need to learn about his exact situation before they could do so.

We agreed, and that afternoon took the motorbike and buzzed down to the hospital.

After making a few enquiries we were soon directed to a public ward on the 2nd floor of this busy building. The poor old boy looked fairly bashed up, and seemed to be almost comatose.

'He looks well out of it,' I told Jum, and we had a brief discussion beside the bed.

'I am here you know!' he said sharply, his angry eyes suddenly opening beneath an old man's frown.

I started chatting to the man while Jum went over to the nurses who were hovering around the ward. She came back after a few minutes and told me that they had assumed I was his buddy, since I looked like a drunken foreigner! She soon put them straight, and as it transpired I actually taught one of their daughters at KPS.

The man's name was Mark and he slowly told us about what had led to his current state. He was an alcoholic, and he had lived in Kalasin for about three years. He was from the USA, existing on his small pension of about 25,000 Thai baht per month. It was almost as much as what I earned for teaching, but I suppose when you are a drunk, that kind of money won't get you far.

He seemed to be angry about the beating, but soon became more interested in how he could get a drink.

The hospital had their own agenda. They had already totted up a decent sized bill for Mark and his injuries. Apparently, the shelter was willing to foot this so long as the man had a passport and was staying in Thailand legally.

I explained this to Mark and he told me that he had his passport on his person. I found this a little odd, as I'd assumed that his attackers would have taken everything. He then produced a dog-eared American passport, and told me he had given just as good as he got. In fact, he was a former Special Forces fighter! I suppose that figured, because Thailand was full of these winners. I didn't even flinch as he regaled me with tales of his exploits in Africa in the '70s.

After saying goodbye, we returned home and popped into the shelter with our news. They seemed happy enough and even asked if we wouldn't mind visiting Mark on a daily basis until he was discharged. This was a little cheeky, but Jum was happy to do so and that was fine by me.

So every day for the next week my wife would visit Mark, and each time she'd bring a small bag of snacks and treats that we paid for ourselves. Jum is a very charitable lady, and even the nurses were scratching their collective heads as they saw her turn up at 2 p.m. daily, just like clockwork. One of them even asked her if this scruffy old man was rich, because she couldn't see any other reason for Jum's behaviour.

After five days I too came along, and could see that Mark was almost ready to be discharged. He had recovered pretty well. I made small talk with him and when Jum was out of earshot he leaned towards me and asked:

'Have the girl bring me a different brand of candy, because these ones truly blow!'

I explained that the 'girl' was my wife and she certainly wasn't to be ordered around. He then regaled me with more tales of his heroics as I politely feigned interest.

Bangkok to Ben Nevis Backwards!

I thought nothing more of it until about a week later, when our paths crossed once more. As I was leaving for school one morning I noticed Mark staring at me through the shelter gates and I wondered how he had managed to wrangle that one out.

When I returned from lessons, Jum told me that the care worker had brought Mark's passport over and wanted us to scan the document for the US embassy. I wondered what was stopping them from doing this themselves, but went ahead anyway.

That evening I was chatting online with a few people on my favourite Thai forum and mentioned Mark to them. One of the moderators on the forum turned out to be a former recruiter for the US military, and he wanted to find out if Mark was the real deal. When I explained that I had a copy of his passport, he asked if I could send him the details. I suppose this was a little sneaky but went ahead anyway.

Over the next week I started chatting to Mark again and discovered that his last three years had been spent going from bottle to bottle and trying to hang on to his marriage. He'd even sired a little boy and despite the way that his wife had treated him, Mark still wanted to try again.

I know there are always two sides to a story, but his seemed all too familiar to my ears. Mark had originally come to Thailand with his life savings and had fallen in love with probably the first lady to pay any real attention to him in decades. He had soon paid for a house to be built for his new love.

Once these funds were depleted so was his value to his new family. Eventually he suspected his new wife of having an affair, and when he finally proved this he was thrown out of the home, despite having paid for the whole lot. He then rented a tiny room and spent his meagre pension on Lao Kao – the cheapest and most potent of Thai spirits.

I felt bad for Mark but what could I do? The last time we spoke I could sense that he had given up, and was back on the bottle.

That evening I checked my emails and was shocked to see that my Thai Visa buddy had sent me one about Mark's military claims. Well blow me down, he really had served in the Special Forces, and was very well decorated!

I decided to go over and see Mark, and even hatched a

little plan to help him regain his dignity.

As I pulled the front gate open I noticed a grey van leaving the shelter. Several of the carers were looking on with forlorn expressions.

I was too late.

About an hour earlier, Mark from Delta Force had taken a sharp knife from the kitchen and opened up a vein whilst taking a warm bath. He'd bled out in less than 20 minutes, according to the carer who'd made the gruesome discovery.

To this day I feel a little responsible for not taking this man at face value.

MEGAN IN OUR GARDEN

The amazing Ambrose Johnson

They say that romance has no bounds and as far as my teacher friend Wannee was concerned, this was definitely the case. In a loveless marriage, Wannee was looking for love in all the wrong places.

At 51 years old, she was still a good looking woman and had more than her fair share of means. Her teacher's salary was over 40,000 Thai baht per month, and in addition she owned a hotel, plus shares in a few other businesses.

But Wannee wanted more; she needed a soul mate, a lover, someone who could see that she still had needs and urges.

Her husband of 25 years had at least three mistresses on the go, and in true Thai fashion he saw these as a proof of his masculinity. He had bought each of them a house, and two of these ladies had given birth to his children. The Thai word for this type of person is 'Mia Noi', meaning Minor wife.

His Major wife had decided that she too would see if the grass really was greener on the other side, and spent all of her spare time trying to find romance on the internet. 'Thai Friend Finder' was her preferred platform, and quite often she would visit the Hall family for some advice on her latest would-be beau. Most of these guys were in their 60s and usually had a cock-and-bull story about how they were looking for that special someone.

One afternoon, whilst in the teachers room, Wannee skipped over with a beaming smile and announced that she had indeed found 'The One'.

I groaned inwardly as she opened up her laptop to show me the profile of a man named Ambrose Johnson. The photos depicted a 40-something man who looked like a Mediterranean type, and in each picture there he was next to the obligatory Lamborghini, yacht, and huge house.

Ambrose apparently lived in Ireland, for tax purposes obviously, and had been widowed a few years previously. He had a 9-year old daughter who really missed her Mummy. Again, this was all textbook scamming stuff, and Ambrose had obviously hit the nail on the head with poor gullible Wannee.

I explained to her that this was a classic scam artist profile, but soon realised that she was having absolutely none of it. She really wanted to believe that this man was her Knight in Shining Armour, and it was clear that nothing I said would make the faintest bit of difference.

As the weeks went on she became closer and closer to Ambrose, and it finally got to the point where I decided to put a stop to this.

One of the best ways to make someone aware of this type

of deceit is to ask if they have had a webcam chat with the scammer.

'Yes, I webcam with Ambrose many times, but never see him.' Wannee explained that these sessions were basically a one-way experience and they would type instead of actually speaking.

I asked why he hadn't actually returned the favour; his excuse was a feeble one. Despite being a self-made millionaire, Mr Johnson couldn't afford a decent webcam. This was more than enough for poor old Wannee to go on, and she absolutely refused to listen to my reasoning.

She then read me some of the romantic prose that had originally swept her off her size 6 feet. It was pure garbage, and I quickly cut and pasted a few lines of it and entered them into the Google search bar. Immediately it was apparent that Ambrose had lifted these sweet words from the internet. I even found a site that warned about romantic scammers who would use these exact words.

Wannee wasn't even mildly concerned, and just as she was about to leave, I asked her to come over that evening and to ask Ambrose for a face to face chat. She could even use our PC. I helped her to write a rather direct message to her would-be beau, explaining that now was the time for him to reveal himself.

So that evening Wannee came over and we dialled in the website details for Thai Friend Finder. She logged in and, surprise surprise, there was no sign of the evil devil.

I sat with Wannee for about ten minutes and then left her to it, as I had a mountain of marking to get through for the next school day. After about another twenty minutes I heard an excited squeal of delight. I could only assume that the elusive Romeo had finally shown up.

'Phil, Phil, he appear, he appear!'

I rushed into the room with Jum and Tom and even Megan in close pursuit, and looked at the happenings on my 20-inch PC screen.

What appeared to be a man of Arabic descent was waving back at me and the rest of the room. I tried to strike up a conversation, but all this character could do was sit down, stand up, wave, and repeat. There was no dialogue other than a few typed words, and this 3-stage visual performance.

Bangkok to Ben Nevis Backwards!

Tom whispered in my ear so not to offend Wannee: 'Dad, this is just a video clip that's used by scammers.' He also pointed out the very clear watermark on the bottom left of the screen. This type of trick is known as a scam bot; the scammer simply gets hold of some video footage and edits it as they wish.

I tried to tell Wannee about our suspicions, but again, she was having none of it. So the weird chat went on for about half an hour, and once Wannee had left I told Jum about my theory. Jum already knew, but Wannee was nothing if not stubborn, so we had no choice but to leave her to it.

About a month later, whilst I was teaching in school, Wannee burst into the room, her face contorted by a mixture of concern and excitement. Once I managed to calm her down she explained that Ambrose planned to come to Thailand, and was bringing his daughter along. He'd stopped in Dubai for a spot of high-powered business, but something had gone terribly wrong.

During a shopping trip, Ambrose was driving his top-of-the-range Mercedes to a retail outlet when there had been an accident. His poor little girl was now in hospital and somehow Ambrose had lost all of his credit cards. He needed some emergency money, and needed it now.

Wannee actually believed this scamming piece of detritus, and all she wanted to know was – how could she send the money?

I was more than dismayed, and after telling her a dozen times about the pattern of these scams, I think she started to realise what may be going on.

Surely a man of his means could simply pick up the phone and get some money wired to his hotel room?

She offered a few workarounds for Mr Johnson but he was having none of it. So I decided to get involved and asked Wannee to call him. Ambrose answered and she passed the phone to me.

Within a few seconds I could tell that I was talking to a Nigerian man. He insisted that he was born in England, but after a few simple questions that he was unable to answer, he hung up.

And that was the end of Ambrose Johnson… well, almost.

About a week later, I checked into my online banking

and was surprised to see that the portal had been blocked. After a few calls to my bank in the UK, I discovered that someone had been trying to access my details.

Ambrose Johnson had a new target.

Thankfully no money had been taken, but that was down to the encryption put in place by NatWest. I wondered how this bugger had managed to almost help himself to my money – and then I remembered something.

The webcam chat.

After a little research I learnt that it is possible to pass a virus into a host computer by way of the ports that are opened when a webcam chat is initiated.

I never mentioned this to Wannee because I think she would have laughed her head off at the irony of the whole thing.

Wannee is still looking for love; I hope that one day she finds it.

KOSUKE

Mustafa's Diamond Mine

I have already talked about this fellow, but there was one incident that I feel needs to be added, for what will become obvious reasons.

Mustafa was a Ghanaian man in his mid-twenties. He was about 6 foot 4, and obviously took pride in his appearance because he was always in the gym and enjoyed showing off his muscles whenever the opportunity presented itself.

Mustafa liked the Thai ladies, and they liked him in return.

He often talked about his uncle's diamond mine back in Ghana, and how he had access to these gems and would one day inherit the whole shebang. I know that Thai ladies are attracted to rich and powerful men, and suspected that this was probably part of the reason why Mustafa was never short of female company.

He started dating a middle aged lady who was obviously smitten with him, and they soon were inseparable. She owned two schools and a string of hotels, so it seemed that my buddy had definitely landed on his size 12 feet.

One day Mustafa told me that he was returning to Ghana for his uncle's funeral (the same man who owned the diamond mine). I had a funny feeling that there was something he was not telling me, and this hunch proved to be correct.

A few days before he was due to leave, Mustafa called me and asked if he could come to my house for a chat. He was at my door less than a minute later, and I could tell that he was in some state of shock.

I told Mustafa that I needed to know exactly what had happened, and he told me a tale that involved a devious little plan:

Mustafa had had enough of Thailand and wanted to return to Ghana. He needed some money to start up a business in Accra but his savings would hardy cover the cost of the single flight. He then hatched up a little scam of his own, one that Ambrose himself would have been impressed by.

He told his rich Thai lady that he would go back to Ghana and would bring back some diamonds worth a fortune. All that she needed to do was to 'lend' him some money for the transaction.

She agreed and once she got his bank details, she wired across the sum of 500,000 Thai baht. This was equivalent to more than two years' teaching salary to Mustafa; he was onto a winner, or so it seemed.

A day later, his girlfriend asked Mustafa to check if those funds had reached his bank account. He went online and was dismayed to learn that they had not. He stalled his girlfriend and now here he was at my house, asking for advice.

He even had the document that she'd used to prove she had wired the money. I examined the paper and although it was definitely from a Thai bank, there was no stamp anywhere to be seen. It appeared that the scammer had been scammed himself! Mustafa looked extremely worried.

He then told me that his girlfriend had called again to say that the Thai police were now involved. If he returned to his apartment, he would be arrested.

I had no doubt that this lady of influence had a few tame policemen and, together, they would extract every last penny from poor Mustafa.

He thanked me for my advice, which was to get the hell out of Dodge, and sped away on his motorbike. To this day I have never seen or even heard from the man again, and I can't help wondering sometimes what became of Mustafa Attobrah...

Chapter 15

A Call for Help / Saying Goodbye to New Friends

There comes a time after you've moved overseas with your family when you take stock and decide whether or not things have worked out as you planned. To be honest, if I had known half of what was lying in wait for the Hall Family, I can say now that I never would have stepped on that plane to India, let alone the one to Thailand! We'd had more ups and downs in 18 months than most families will experience in their entire lives. But here we were, and apart from a few scars and some mixed memories, we were doing okay.

For us, this day of reckoning was sometime during March 2013. I was approaching the end of my first year as a teacher at KPS and I was loving the job, despite some of the obstacles that I had to deal with. I had made adjustments and was developing into a decent teacher.

Jum was happy enough but I felt that she was somewhat bored. Tom was having the best time of his life, and the only real issue that I could see was the level of education offered by KPS. He was shortly going to move up to M4 and had three years left before Thai University would beckon. I had no doubt that he would enjoy his time here in Thailand, and would probably find a decent job by the time he graduated, but there was an underlying issue.

At some point it was likely that Tom Hall would want to come back to the UK and possibly find meaningful employment. His Thai Bachelor's degree wouldn't carry much weight back in Europe, and most blue chip companies would see it as a meaningless piece of paper that probably had less value than a few A levels.

When you consider that he would be at least 23 years old at this point – because it takes five years to qualify from a Thai University – it wouldn't be much to show for that amount of schooling.

Of course, if he chose to stay in Thailand there would be no such issues, but I felt he should have the freedom of choice.

At this point in time, as a 15-year old boy, of course he couldn't make that choice because all he wanted to do was have fun, and there was plenty of that to be had right here.

Jum and I talked about this dilemma, and the topic of International schooling came up more than once. These privately funded institutions run a number of syllabuses, the IGSE being probably the most desirable for those hailing from the UK. They employed proper teachers, not TEFL instructors like yours truly, and usually had boarding facilities.

The main issue with us moving Tom to an International School were the somewhat steep fees. Typically, an International school would charge somewhere in the region of one million baht per year.

This equates to around £20,000! My salary was only about £6,000...

On the other hand, I had recently found another way to earn money which was proving to be very fruitful indeed.

One of my friends on a Thai forum had suggested I try my hand at article writing.

Also known as copywriting or content writing, this entailed producing articles around the 500-word mark on a variety of topics. An Indian company had offered me 300 Thai baht for each successfully submitted piece and although I was slow in the beginning, I soon managed to pick up the pace. After about a month I was bringing in an extra 60,000 Thai baht per month!

I managed to write my articles in between lessons and during the evenings and weekends. This had tripled our income, and for once we could actually put some of this aside for savings. Although our total annual income wasn't enough to cover the typical International school fees, it

A Call for Help / Saying Goodbye to New Friends

would certainly help.

After scouring the Kalasin and Kohn Kaen areas for International schools we eventually found one with terms and conditions that we could just about manage. We visited the school and to be honest, whilst not spectacular, it was far better than KPS. The fees were around 50,000 Thai baht per month and so long as I wrote my socks off, we could afford this plus our own rent and outgoings. Tom seemed, happy although he would miss his KPS buddies. All of the lessons were taught in English and most of the teachers were from the UK.

After the grand tour, we found a nice seafood restaurant and stuffed ourselves silly whilst discussing the future. We'd just about agreed that we should give Thailand one more year, with Tom in the International school and me teaching and writing, when my phone started to ring.

It was coming from Mum and Dad's house phone. The ensuing conversation would change our lives forever.

'Phil, it's Mum, they have taken my Colin away!'

'Calm down Mum, please tell me what happened, and try not to cry!' I pleaded with my mother, because I knew what I was about to be told would not be pleasant, but I needed to hear the facts.

Mum told me that Dad's condition had worsened to the point where he would wet the bed every night, get up at odd hours and even leave the house at 2 or 3am. Eventually she had suffered what is known as a 'carer's breakdown', and a neighbour had alerted her doctor.

I learnt that the carers who visited twice a day had been told some months earlier by Mum that they were no longer required. This had been a misjudgement on her part, and each day thereafter was a battle of the wills against a very stubborn old man in the midst of Vascular Dementia. For instance, he would throw his food across the room, wake up and watch TV at 4am, and leave the volume on full as he returned to his bed.

Mum was 70 years old herself and not in the best of health. Her heavy smoking had damaged her blood vessels and she found it very hard to walk. Although Dad's mind had all but been wiped out, he was still physically fit, and nimble enough to run rings around her.

As Mum told me about her living hell I started to realise

Bangkok to Ben Nevis Backwards!

that our own plans for living in Thailand would have to be put on ice.

I could have easily made a few whimpering noises and got back to our own version of reality, but that wasn't what I was made of. I had always tried to do my best for my family, and even though my immediate one may have suffered indirectly, it was still a version of 'doing the right thing' – that overused cliché people seemed to use on a daily basis when it suited them.

So, back to our dilemma...

I looked at Jum and Tom and they both agreed that we were needed back in Scotland. So that was it, no more teaching, no more chilled out life – at least for now. Mum had been there for me throughout my life, and now was the time to pay back her kindness.

When we lived in South Africa Dad would work away from home for weeks on end. He had a job as a meteorologist in the Orange Free State, some 700 miles away from where we lived. Dad could only come home on the odd weekend, and as a result Mum pretty much brought us up for 4 or 5 years.

Now Mum needed my help and I was happy to be able to return the favour.

She explained that there was no way that she could cope with Dad being at home, even with my help.

I was amazed at how quickly my wife had agreed to the move, especially considering her last contact with Mum and Dad. Jum's own family had acted like prize bastards, and now mine were in need of assistance, she never hesitated – and Tom had also been very mature about the whole thing: 'We need to help Nanny and that is what we will do.'

I was so proud of both of them!

I wrote down my new list of objectives:

1. Speak to KPS school
2. Tell International School that Tom will not be starting
3. Make arrangements for Megan
4. Look at job situation in Fort William
5. Send Megan back
6. Say goodbye to friends
7. Contact school in Fort William
8. Leave Thailand

On paper this seemed pretty easy, but I knew that it would be anything but. Our funds were not exactly healthy but we had enough to go back, and hopefully there would be work in Fort William – where I knew the schooling would certainly be of a higher standard than KPS, and probably the International School too.

When I told Ajarn Kwan that I would not be teaching the next year he seemed to take it well, especially when I explained the family issue.

'Well Philip, you must look after your parents and Tom will have a better education back in the UK.' He was right on both counts.

I started to think about how I felt about Dad being in care and realised that it would be a huge shock when I finally came to terms with the fact that he would never come home again. As a child I would have nightmares about my parents being killed in all sorts of horrific ways, but this was worse. Nothing exciting, and certainly not even rare, but Vascular Dementia had all but done for Colin Hall – and he was still very much alive.

The last four or five weeks in Thailand were spent enjoying the country and all that it had to offer, because I knew that we wouldn't be back for a long time. Jum's mum turned up out of the blue one day, and stayed with us for a few weeks. I half expected Jum to kick off about the way that she had been treated after the stabbing, but true to form she welcomed her Mum with open arms. I wouldn't say that they exactly bonded over that period, but they certainly weren't at daggers drawn, if you'll excuse the pun.

Tom was rarely at home as he made the most of the time left in Kalasin; it was clear that he would miss this place very much indeed.

I said goodbye to my one thousand students and fellow teachers, and tried not to dwell on the fact that I may never teach again. Life is full of opportunities, but the older we become, the fewer of them appear.

Would I be going back to a dull and soulless IT job? Well, I was soon served up a healthy dose of reality when I contacted my old buddies at PepsiCo to test the waters. Richard Jones was still the boss, and I foolishly emailed

Bangkok to Ben Nevis Backwards!

him with a quick enquiry, as I had heard that there were a few vacancies on the service desk. He replied in the negative, and even told me that he knew that I would fail and was surprised that I lasted so long.

I shouldn't have been surprised but I was pretty mad. More angry at my own naivety, really.

We arranged for Megan to be tested for Rabies and, once the blood sample had been okayed by a vet in Brussels, we sorted out her travel details. It would cost around £1000, but we didn't really have a choice because Megan was one of us and would always be a family member. I often recoil with distaste when I hear about families who simply leave their dogs behind when moving away or back home. How can these people even sleep at night? Dogs really do bond with their owners and, true to their pack mentality, they consider us to be one of their own.

MEGAN IN HER CAGE

About two weeks after that phone call from Mum we had booked and paid for our own flights, and began to sell the entire contents from our latest home. We had loads of decent furniture, a widescreen TV, a drum set, all kinds of kitchen appliances and a couple of motorbikes to get rid of.

A Call for Help / Saying Goodbye to New Friends

The lot was snapped up by one of Jum's new friends, and I suppose we got a fair price, all things considered.

The day that we took Megan to the airport in Kohn Kaen was a sad one, and it brought home the fact that we really were saying goodbye to yet another stage of our complicated lives. Jum was in pieces, but I did my best to reassure her that this was the right thing, the *only* thing that we could do.

About one week before we left Thailand I called Mum for an update and was pretty disheartened by the conversation that followed.

'But Phil, where will you stay?'

Mum didn't appear to be keen on us staying with her. This wasn't what I wanted to hear.

I explained that we had nowhere to go and we intended to stay at 2 Glen Spean Park for the foreseeable future. She seemed a little more distant than the previous phone call, and her lack of warmth pretty much knocked me off my feet. We had dropped everything, and now Mum was closing the door, just when we needed her as much as I thought she had needed us. Megan was already in the UK, and we had all but burnt our bridges here in Kalasin.

Eventually Mum accepted the situation, and I asked her to write down the date that we would be arriving. She hadn't seen Dad since that morning when he had been taken away, and didn't even know where he was staying.

We had a very hard time ahead of us and, not for the first time, I cursed my luck and wondered why life was sucking so much at this point in time.

A few days later we bid Kalasin a fond farewell and Jum promised her mother that she would soon be sending money back... some things never change.

We spent the last four days in the seaside resort of Pattaya and did our best to relax, even though all I could think about was the Scottish weather and the uncertain welcome that awaited us.

The mini break soon ended and, as our taxi pulled up outside of Suvarnabhumi International Airport, I felt that familiar heavy feeling in my heart as the latest Thai adventure was brought to an abrupt end.

Chapter 16

Homeward Bound

It felt as if we had been out of the UK for the best part of a decade, but as we left the M25 to join the M1 and headed North, I realised it had been just 18 months since we'd said goodbye to my parents up in Roy Bridge. So much had happened in that time, both in India and Thailand – and of course, back in Lochaber. A stark reminder that no matter how involved you may be with life, the world simply does not stand still; despite the best intentions in the world, bad things can and will happen to those around you, including the ones you love the most. Some of these bad things are unavoidable, and some are even caused by those closest to us.

So just a year and a half after we had set off to India with our worldly possessions and little white dog following close behind, here we were, back again and fairly worse for wear – some of us literally scarred by the whole experience, but although not defeated, we certainly had a different outlook on life than previously.

Jum, Tom and Megan seemed to be totally zonked out thanks to the long flight and extended stay in the kennels– well, for Megan anyway – so I had a fair bit of time to do what I seemed to do the best: think about how the blazes we would deal with the next chapter in our lives.

When we left Mum and Dad back in 2011, I knew that someday I would get a phone call that would stop me in my tracks. Life would have to be put on hold for the greater good of my family, and that thought never ever left my mind. It was as if the reminder of this inevitable event was

Bangkok to Ben Nevis Backwards!

looming over us wherever we were in the world.

They say that your family always remains in your heart, and no matter how far you may roam, they are always just a few thoughts away.

I used to refer to our own personal tie as the 'Shadow of Ben Nevis', and despite the mountain being properly dwarfed by the likes of Mount Everest and other heavyweights, this Scottish peak had a spiritual reach that crossed oceans and continents like no other.

So the call had come, about 6 weeks earlier now, and although it wasn't the showstopper that I had expected, the news was more than enough to put our own personal plans into a spin that still hadn't really slowed down.

After 18 months of looking after my mentally ill father, Mum had finally succumbed to a condition known as 'Carer's Breakdown'. This comes about when the carer hits a wall that is pretty much unsurmountable. Despite their best efforts, it becomes apparent to them that they can longer help their loved one without external help. In Mum's case it was probably inevitable, but came as a shock nonetheless, especially to Christina Hall herself.

I called her every week whilst abroad and there was definitely a pattern emerging with regards to Dad's condition, and further deterioration was inevitable.

I suppose I realised that he was soon going to be going into full time care after Mum described the night when she awoke to find the front door of the house wide open, with Dad and Jock 2 nowhere to be seen. It had been a pretty stormy night as well, so finding out that your dear husband, bereft of pretty much all of his mental capacity, had decided to go on a moonlight stroll with a one-year-old West Highland Terrier wasn't exactly the news you wanted to hear.

He hadn't got far. The lady across the road, Norma, had heard a commotion in her kitchen and when she got out of bed and made her way to that room, she got the surprise of her life!

Poking around her cupboards and muttering something about baked beans, was Colin Raymond Hall. Butt naked as the day he was born, and not bothered in the slightest.

When he noticed the red haired Scottish lady screaming at him to get out, he simply smiled and exited the scene, with one tin of soup in his hands and a confused-looking

Westie following close behind.

He did stop before he reached the gate and asked Norma about 'the strange old woman in my house', before returning to number 2 with his spoils.

As far as Mum was concerned, this was the last straw. She asked herself – what would have happened if he had wandered onto the main road? Or perhaps taken a stroll towards the river and ended up drowning in the bloody thing?

Every time we had spoken on the phone from Thailand, Mum had seemed to be handling things okay. However, she had complained about the pair of carers who had 'stuck their noses in our business', and after a few months she had sent them packing. But it was apparent to me, even 6,000 miles away, that Mum was covering things up and making the best of it.

Dad's condition had gotten a lot worse. She would wake up in the early hours of the morning to find him watching the same TV show over and over again. Eventually he no longer even did this; his days were spent simply drifting through the house and occasionally shouting unintelligible words at Mum.

So the day that the ambulance came to take my Father away was not only the saddest in the life of Mum, it was also the light at the end of that two-year tunnel that had all but destroyed her.

When she told me that Dad had 'gone away' I cried for at least an hour. Okay, I did this in private, but my grieving was deeply genuine, and I knew that he would never be coming back.

I decided to stop for some food and a little rest. As I parked the car outside the motorway services I joined the rest of my little throng and got some much needed sleep.

My mind was still in Thailand and as I drifted off, the last 18 months whizzed through my tired subconscious in a way that can only be brought on by international travel mixed with fatigue and stress. The Indian flop had lasted less than four weeks, and the decision to try our luck in Thailand had certainly not been plain sailing. Yet just as things were finally on track, they had been derailed once more.

Eventually my snoring must have woken the rest of the car's sleeping beauties and I stirred as Jum and Tom closed the doors behind them and walked Megan around the car park area. We were still at least eight hours away from Spean Bridge, and I had no idea what lay ahead. I imagined the worst, and wondered what on earth we would do for work and money as I reminded myself of the lack of jobs in Lochaber.

In Thailand I had held a position of respect and interacted with over 1,000 people every week. This had worked wonders for my confidence, but how could I follow that with my next number? A low-paid mundane job in IT, if I was lucky! Well, at least Tom would be back in the UK education system, so it wasn't all bad. But we would be living with Mum – who smoked like a trooper. With Tom and Jum's asthma conditions, things would not be easy.

Then I thought about my father and wondered if he would even recognise me. I had waited all of my life to finally get a job overseas and somehow gain his approval. Now, selfishly, I had managed it, and the poor old bloke wouldn't even know who I was.

I felt proud that my wife and son had not even grumbled about this life changing move. They'd had enough about them to step up to the plate, and I loved them for this selfless characteristic.

So we cracked on with the rest of the journey, and just before nightfall we pulled up in the drive of number 2 Glenspean Park once more – to add yet another chapter to our lives.

Jock 2 was straight out of the kitchen and upon us as we exited the car, and for some reason I was surprised to see how grown up this noisy little bugger had become. He must have had a hell of a time over the last 18 months, and if dogs could talk, his memoirs would be some read!

Megan and Jock instantly bonded, or re-bonded, and as they tore around the large garden I could make out the shape of Mum by the kitchen window. I walked towards the house to greet her.

'Hello dear!' Mum's voice was crackled and straight away I could see that she had aged considerably since I had last seen her.

Homeward Bound

As I hugged her, I could sense that things were not okay, not at all. The house had a funky smell about it that I couldn't recognise at first, and I knew that she probably needed a wash herself. Old age is such a cruel leveller. It sneaks up on you, and although I still had a few decades to go, I hated this stage of life with a passion.

It was a lot to take in, and instead of sitting down for a much needed catch-up I emptied the car and did everything I could to delay the inevitable. Eventually I decided to bottle out, and slunk off to the spare room for a sleep.

When I opened the door I was hit by a smell that nearly knocked me off my feet. Dad had been using this room for the past 18 months and it was apparent from what Mum had told me that the poor old guy had long since lost control of his bladder. The windows were closed and the radiator was belting out heat, even in late April.

I opened the windows up and turned the heat off, wondering what despair had gone on in this small room.

Mum must have read my mind, because she was stood in the doorway and gave me a sad look as she explained how she didn't have the strength to clean the carpets that had obviously been soaked with urine in the past.

I felt both ashamed and angry at the same time. How could life be so cruel, to take away a person's dignity in such a short time? Surely death was a better option? And why had Mum been forced to endure this all alone?

In Thailand, families did things differently. Elderly parents were looked after, even revered, by their families – old people's homes simply did not exist. It was the same all over Asia and probably in Africa and South America as well. Only the so-called First World countries carried out these practices.

Okay, Jum's people were certainly not going to win any prizes for Family of the Year, but even they would shudder at the thought of their own being carted off to God knows where for the rest of their natural lives.

I sat down with Mum and listened over a glass of malt whiskey as she brought me up to date. I could see that her hands were shaking, and even the clouds of cigarette smoke billowing my way didn't really faze me as she spoke of the hardship endured since we had left.

Bangkok to Ben Nevis Backwards!

JUM AND MEGAN IN LOCHABER

I noticed that Mum was gulping down the whiskey and to distract her I decided to ask her about where Dad was currently staying, but almost immediately I wished that I hadn't. The pain in her eyes was apparent and I couldn't imagine what this proud woman must have gone through since we'd left.

Mum was all about putting a brave face on things; she would do almost anything to prevent the outside world from finding out what went on behind closed doors. Perhaps this was why she had been mortified when the two carers had starting paying visits. Dad may have been in the middle stages of Vascular Dementia, but she was buggered if anybody else needed to know this terrible fact.

Apparently he had been taking Jock on very long walks alongside the busy road that passed through Roy Bridge, and had quite often become lost. Mum was almost anticipating the day when the police would drop by to tell her that Colin Hall had been involved in an argument with an 18-wheeler and had come off worse, and that all that was left of wee Jock was his collar and some fluff.

Thankfully that day had never come and now that Dad

was 'safe' somewhere yet to be disclosed to yours truly, it would never arrive – or at least not in those grisly circumstances.

Mum and Dad had lived the dream, travelling the world with their small family and eventually coming to Fort William to see out their days. The dream had lasted nearly a decade, and during this time Mum continued to write books and Dad turned a huge forest-like swamp of a garden into a beautiful display of lawns and flowers.

I suppose I knew that Dad had really started on the road to his demise when I brought up a guitar pedal for him to repair. Dad was genius-like with the soldering iron and as an electrical engineer who had served for more than 20 years in the REME, it had pretty much been his tool of choice. I was hopeless with my hands, and when the poor old pedal had stopped working I knew one man that could fix this in a jiffy. So what if he was passed his sell-by date? This was a simple re-soldering of a couple of dry joints that would be a walk in the park.

Except that it wasn't.

I can still remember watching as he looked at the innards of the pedal as if they were from Mars.

'Dad, what's the problem?' I asked in a childlike way.

'I can't do this,' he replied and, placing the soldering iron onto the circuit board, he left the shed.

By the time I had reached the pedal, the heat of the iron had sliced the board in two. It was definitely broken now, even if not before!

That was the day that I knew my Father was going to a place where I couldn't reach him anymore. The doctors had told Mum to expect the worst, and less than three years later he was committed to a mental health facility somewhere near Inverness.

That was all Mum would say, and each time I broached the subject, she would tell me that she couldn't remember the name of the hospital. Over the next week or so, I asked less and less until I didn't even talk about Dad when Mum was about.

The problem was that Mum too had altered so much from the person she used to be. Physically she was struggling to walk for more than a few minutes at a time, but mentally, things were even worse.

Bangkok to Ben Nevis Backwards!

One evening she was telling me about the train that passed the house three or four times a day. It was en-route to Glasgow, or on its way to Fort William via Roy Bridge station, and would sometimes stop at the end of the garden. I had assumed this was to wait for the train in the next direction to pass by safely, but according to Mum they were stopping to allow the passengers to take photos of the house.

I asked why they would be interested, and Mum's face beamed with pride when she told me they were taking photos of the famous author's house. I was about to crack up with laughter when I realised that she was being 100% serious. Poor Mum was showing signs of dementia herself. What had happened to my parents in such a short time?

A little after this revelation I was scrabbling around in the spare bedroom for a book to read when I stumbled upon a large Jiffy bag envelope with a familiar address on the front. I looked inside and found a bunch of official-looking documents, with a ring box concealed within.

When I opened the box my heart kind of skipped a beat. In my hand was my 'lost' wedding ring! The very same ring I had mislaid the day before we flew to India. Mum had found the ring a few months later and sent it to me in Thailand. Needless to say, the ring never arrived and, along with some important Thai documents, was never seen again.

Until now, that is.

The truth sank in as I realised that Mum had never sent the ring.

I was so happy to have it back again, but when I asked Mum about the envelope and the anguish that we had gone through she seemed pretty unconcerned.

'Never mind Dear, at least now you have it!'

In fact, she seemed almost bored by the topic.

So we had been at Mum's house for a fortnight and some things had developed nicely, whilst others had not. We had enrolled Tom at Lochaber High School and he was enjoying it as far as we could see. Jum and I had signed on to Social Services, and although jobs were thin on the ground at least we had some semblance of money coming in. Megan and Jock were firm friends, and this was all good, except for two things.

Homeward Bound

I still had no idea where Dad was staying, and Mum still wasn't letting on how ill *she* really was.

I suppose what I was trying to do was think of a plan, as I always did, to fix this terrible situation. Except this time, I couldn't. Nobody could.

Dad was gone and Mum was in a place where I couldn't really reach her. I often heard her making a humming noise when alone; she didn't seem to even realise that she was doing this. We had returned from an idyllic life and plunged into the midst of a disaster zone that I had no chance of controlling.

Jum and I pitched in with keeping the house tidy, and she got a housekeeping job at the local hotel. There were no jobs for me in Lochaber, but I managed to qualify for a carer's allowance and took my new role very seriously. After all, it was Mum who had looked after me for so many years, so why wouldn't I be happy to return the compliment?

Mum did her best to keep the kitchen as tidy as possible, but after a few days I noticed the mini-dishwasher on the countertop. This was jam-packed with dishes and cutlery, and I could see that it was being used as a storage device also. The problem was that it took up loads of space between the sink and the cooker, and I decided that I'd shift it into the garage and free up the countertop.

I put this suggestion to Mum and she seemed a little reticent to agree with me.

'Oh, I don't know dear, I like the little dishwasher and it makes things easier for me.'

I explained that we were here now and would take over the cleaning duties for the foreseeable future. She eventually backed down and I unplumbed the device and retired it with full honours to the garage.

The surface beneath the dishwasher was pretty manky, so I spent the best part of an hour cleaning it up and decided to cook a decent dinner to take full advantage of the newly liberated space. After dinner I quickly washed up all of the plates, noticing that Mum kept looking forlornly over to where the little dishwasher used to be.

A few days later I was going to wash up the breakfast plates, but I was too late – they had already been done. I went to check the cupboards and, although nice and dry, the state of the plates and the knives and forks was pretty abysmal. Mum had obviously given the washing up her best efforts, but the results were not exactly world class. I decided to let it ride, and re-washed them as quickly as possible.

We had a decent lunch thanks to Jum and the Thai food she lovingly created – made all three of us feel a little homesick. Okay, we had only lived in Thailand for about 15 months, but the place was still very much in our hearts and minds.

'Dad, will we ever go back to Thailand?'

Tom would ask me this question every few days and although he was making the best of it at his new school, it was clear that he really missed his old friends and lifestyle. In Thailand we had a very different type of family life, and freedom was certainly the key to a happy Hall family. Life was lived to the full and we seldom spent the evenings in the house watching TV. There, eating out and meeting up with friends was the order of the day.

After clearing up the plates and stacking them by the sink I decided to take Tom out for a little fishing trip. We had fished often back in Isaan, and a fishing trip in Kalasin usually involved a small hut with food and beer being supplied on demand –we even managed to catch some fish.

At least Roy Bridge had a small river with a few trout knocking about, and about an hour later we returned empty-handed, but a little happier nonetheless.

I did my best to explain to Tom that we would indeed return to that life in Thailand, but for now Nanny needed us more.

'Where is Grandad?' Tom asked, and I had to tell him that I wasn't sure but would find out and we would go and see him in the near future.

I decided to confront Mum about Dad's whereabouts.

As I entered the kitchen I noticed she was doing the washing up. The poor old dear was almost bent over double and was making the best of a bad job, bless her! Despite me and Jum asking Mum to take a back seat as far as the washing up and general cleaning was concerned, this stubborn old lady was having none of it!

I slipped through the kitchen unnoticed, realisng that Mum's independence was extremely important to her and I'd been an idiot to try and assume control — as if I ever could!

Homeward Bound

I waited a little while and heard her go into her bedroom for an afternoon nap. Then I rushed out to the garage and reinstalled the pesky dishwasher as quickly as possible. A little later I was enjoying a cup of tea and admiring the view of the mountains as Mum came into the kitchen; as she sat down she gave me a winning smile and said,

'I see the little dishwasher has returned from his travels then, Philip!'

Every morning I woke up with some semblance of resolve, but as soon as I saw Mum sat at the kitchen table, her favourite place, on her tenth cigarette of the day, all hope went out of the window. Despite her love for my son, she would still smoke when he was in the kitchen; even though his asthma-related cough was the worse I'd ever heard it.

'Phil, this is my house and I will do whatever I like!'

There was a form of logic in there somewhere and I knew that whatever the future brought, we would have to move out at some point.

Jum was fast becoming frustrated with the whole set up and one day, after a particularly fraught morning, I decided that I had to man up and lay down the law. So I did what I do best and made up a list that I hoped would change things for the better.

It went a little like this:

1. Find out where Dad is staying/being held
2. Convince Mum to visit him
3. Visit Dad
4. Start looking for places to live
5. Get a carer package set up for Mum.
6. If all else fails – bugger off to Thailand

So on this particular morning, as I greeted my mother in the smoke-ridden kitchen, already making those humming noises, I finally grew a pair and got down to business.

'Mum, where the hell is Dad?'

It had taken nearly three weeks but finally I had found my stones, and Mum knew that I would not back down until she delivered the goods. She took an extra-long drag on her Superking cigarette and looked me straight in the eye.

'He is at New Craig's Hospital, Phil.'

Bangkok to Ben Nevis Backwards!

I was surprised how easy this was, and when I asked her if she would come with me to visit him she nodded, and that was that.

Of course, I hold some of the blame because I knew that the next time I saw my father, it would be a terrible, heartbreaking event. Well... who could feel any different? Watching your heroes die will never be easy to deal with.

The rest of the day was a blur. Once I had called the mental hospital and arranged for a visit the next day, everything else seemed to phase out, as if it wasn't really happening. Mum smoked even more than usual, and when Tom came home from school Jum and I took the dogs for a walk and had a little catch-up chat.

Since we had arrived, Mum would not let us into her room for a much-needed tidy up. Although I hate to say this, the bed sheets obviously needed washing and the rest of the bedroom was in dire need of some TLC. The problem was that Mum never *ever* left the house, and was always one step away from her room.

So between us we decided that Jum would clean the room whilst Mum and I visited Dad in Inverness.

The trip would take at least three or four hours including driving time, and that would be enough to clean the house three times over – so one bedroom would be no problem whatsoever.

We still needed to talk about whether or not we could stay with Mum for the long term, and Jum suggested that perhaps we could talk about a care package for her.

This was all well and good, but first of all I needed to see my Dad.

The rest of the day dragged, and I got the feeling that Mum was dreading tomorrow even more than I was. What version of Colin Hall would be waiting for us at New Craigs? Would he even know who we were?

And why was Mum so bloody reticent to visit her husband of 50 years?

I knew that this would probably be the most challenging day of my life and to be honest, I wasn't even sure that I could do this without some kind of a breakdown!

Then I thought about the last 18 months and how my mother had dealt with his deterioration with hardly any help from the outside world. What must she have had to go

Homeward Bound

through every waking moment? I knew that I couldn't have matched her courage and strength, not for one minute.

But now I had to be strong enough to help Mum make this journey, and although I knew that Dad was probably beyond all help, I could help wondering against all knowledge whether he would ever come home again? Even just for a single day?

I said goodnight to Mum and went to bed.

Mum must have known the anguish that I was going through, and she left me alone to my thoughts. I had some hideous dreams that night; I can't even bear to write down the scenarios that appeared in my mind.

The next day I was up very early and for some reason decided to wash Mum's little car. We were due at New Craigs at midday; the journey would easily take ninety minutes. So I had asked Mum to be ready at 10am, just in case she was dragging her feet.

By 9am there was no sign of her, so I knocked on the bedroom door and heard her stirring.

'Mum, it's time for you to get up, we leave in one hour!'

'Okay dear, there's no rush,' she replied, but I could tell that she was really not into this visit at all.

By ten o'clock Mum was still at the breakfast table in her PJ's and I started to get a little irritated. I rushed her along and, begrudgingly, she sloped off to get changed.

Eventually, at about 11.15, we were in the car and on our way to see Dad at New Craigs Hospital. As we passed the Commando Memorial just outside Spean Bridge on the Achintore Road to Inverness, I started to revisit my dreams. They didn't make pleasant viewing.

I've never experienced a car journey with so little conversation, and by the time we were in Fort Augustus, neither mother nor son had uttered a single word.

'Lovely day isn't it?' The silence was shattered by my attempt to make conversation, but the truth was that we had other things on our minds.

As we passed Loch Oich I noticed a shop with a rather odd name and said it out loud: 'The Well of the Seven Heads Store...'

'What was that dear?' Mum asked, and I told her about the shop's name.

Bangkok to Ben Nevis Backwards!

Before I knew it, Mum was telling me all about the origins of this name, and I was more than a little surprised to learn how it came about. Now I forget the exact details, but this old tale made my dreams from last night seem like CBBC by comparison.

Back in 1663, one Alexander MacDonald and his brother were killed by clan members. This went unpunished until the Edinburgh Privy Council sent orders to avenge these deaths; as a result, the seven people responsible were done away with. In fact, they were decapitated, and each head was to be presented to the boss of the MacDonald clan.

But the executioners were in a bit of a state after the deed was done, so the guy who had carried out the chopping decided to stop at a nearby spring to wash the heads until they were nice and presentable – or at least a little less bloody.

The heads were duly presented, and ever since, the well has been known as 'Tobar nan Ceann' – Gaelic for 'The Well of the Heads'.

A truly gruesome story, and some believe that this well still holds mystical powers.

As we drove past Loch Ness I thought about the story, and my own dream from the previous night started to come back to life.

Dad had once told me about something that happened to him when he was going out with Mum back in South Uist. He was a young 20-something in the British Army back then, and Mum was a school teacher still living with her parents in Kilpheder, South Uist. He used to drive from the army camp on the other side of the tiny island to spend time with his sweetheart every evening.

There was an old legend doing the rounds at the time and it went something like this:

Many centuries ago the Devil used to scour the roads of the Outer Hebrides looking for souls to steal. His coach and horses could be heard from miles away between the hours of 2am and 4am. Anybody found wandering the island at this ungodly hour would be taken away and never heard of again. Apparently quite a few old drunks went this way, and their relatives would pray for their souls every Sunday.

One particularly hideous night, the Devil was up to his usual tricks when he discovered a young woman who was seemingly lost, and he decided to swoop down on her – except this time his coachman decided to intervene, and pleaded with the devil to spare the young lady.

A huge argument ensued, and the girl managed to escape with her life. The devil was really angry about losing the fresh young soul, and immediately fired his coachman. But Satan was not as bad as people made out, and before leaving the island forever he told his ex-coachman that so long as he could find 1000 souls on his own, he would be reinstated.

Ever since that fateful night, between the hours of two and four in the morning, on the Kilpheder road just by the machair, the devil's coachman wanders the road and any car that passes, so long as there is a single driver at the wheel with no passengers, the coachman appears in the rear seat for the duration of the journey. If the driver looks in the mirror, just for a second, the coachman will take his soul for the devil's collection.

This was a nice little slice of folklore and in my dream, Dad was on that road at precisely 3 a.m. and, true to form, the devil's coachman made an appearance in the back seat of his old Hillman Imp. This was a tiny car from the 1960s, so I assumed the coachman was no giant.

My Dad could sense that he was not alone and, against his better judgement, he glanced in the rear view mirror – to see the demon grinning back at him.

Dad pulled over and pleaded with the coachman to spare his soul. But the demon was having none of it. So Dad, pretty desperate by now, tried to make a deal and offered this to the coachman:

'How about this: if I beat you at cards, you can take my soul, but not until my life has been lived to the full?'

After defeating the demon in a few hands of rummy, Dad's favourite, they struck a deal and Dad escaped with his soul intact.

He went on to live his life to the full.

This much was true because Dad gave 100% to every aspect of his life, and we certainly were grateful for the way this remarkable man did exactly that.

So fast forward to about 50-odd years later and, just as agreed, the devil's coachman came for my Dad's soul. He took it one summer's night, but instead of dying in his

Bangkok to Ben Nevis Backwards!

sleep, Dad managed to wake up just as he always did, around 6am the next day.

But this time, something was wrong. As he jumped out of bed and looked into the mirror, a stranger was staring right back at him.

He forgot to walk his beloved dog that morning, even though it had been part of his routine for the last X years. His words were slurred and his memory had faded. Colin Hall was still breathing, but this once meticulous man had somehow been transformed into a shell, with no clue how to even brush his teeth properly.

Of course, Vascular Dementia does not work in such a severe way; rather it creeps up on the victim and takes their dignity away, piece by piece.

Surely death would be kinder?

My Dad was eventually diagnosed with Vascular Dementia, but in my dream, something far more sinister had happened. I also thought about how the word 'Devil' spelt backwards was 'Lived'. Dementia is certainly the work of demons, because who else could dream up such a living hell for both the sufferer and their friends and family?

I wondered how much truth was in that old wives' tale, and just as I was going to share my little nightmare with Mum, I realised that we had just arrived outside the New Craigs Hospital.

We were here.

We must have sat in silence for at least five minutes until Mum stubbed her cigarette out and spoke up.

'Okay then dear, let's go.'

We slowly left the car and went to see Dad.

Chapter 17

What We've Become

We soon found the ward where Dad was supposed to be staying and as we entered the narrow corridor I could hear what seemed to be the sounds of people who had lost their minds. There were low moans, high pitched screams and every single noise in between.

As we approached the reception area I looked around to see if Dad was amongst these poor buggers – surely we had come to the wrong place? I couldn't see a single soul who was compos mentis and pretty soon I was fearing the very worst.

After about five minutes a stern-faced nurse appeared and told us in a soft voice to wait in a small room while she went to fetch Dad.

Mum and I sat in stony silence, both staring at the floor. It really was as if we were in Satan's waiting room, the atmosphere was that tense.

Suddenly, the calm was rudely interrupted as the door swung open and we were faced with a shuffling wreck of a man. His hair was almost standing on end and there was a large cut on his left cheek. His eyes were wild and he was sobbing like an infant who had been told to go to bed for being naughty.

This was my Dad. This poor man who clearly had lost his marbles was looking on forlornly, and I could do was cry my bloody eyes out.

Mum was in a similar state as she kept repeating the same phrase over and over again: 'Oh Colin, Colin, what has happened to you, my poor darling?'

The nurse left us to it and as the door closed I did my best to give poor Dad a cuddle. His body was bony and he was trembling; he simply stood there as I tried to guide him towards a chair. When I looked into my father's eyes I could see no recognition, just a dull blue mess where a lively stare used to be.

I suppose I cried for a good few minutes, but when the door swung open again I tried to pull myself together.

'Tea or Coffee?'

I must have answered because a few minutes later a trolley appeared with tea, coffee and biscuits. Finally Mum started trying to speak to Dad. She held one of his hands as I poured our drinks.

The door opened again and an odd-looking woman with large bandage on her head walked into the room, picked up the plate of biscuits and promptly disappeared with her loot. One of those bizarre moments that happens when you least expect it!

Mum and I saw the funny side of it as we chuckled for a few seconds; this was the saddest moment of my life by a long way, but at least we could thank God for our sense of humour.

However, right at that moment, God was very far from this place.

The nurse brought us up to date. Apparently his cut was the result of him picking at a small shaving scab, which had progressed into a melanoma of sorts. She promised that it would be looked at as soon as possible, and tried her best to reassure Mum and I that he was in the best place for him.

So what exactly was New Craigs Hospital? I could see that this ward was for dementia patients, but how long had these poor buggers been here?

Apparently it was a kind of holding tank for those who were yet to be placed in a care home. Care homes in Scotland have limited spaces and sometimes patients have to wait an awfully long time before they can move in. The hospital was a good 2 hours away from Fort William, so we would have to start looking into moving Dad into one nearer to us, sooner rather than later. We could discuss these plans once we'd recovered from this visit.

Dad was obviously under some heavy sedatives, because after his cup of tea, he was 'away with the fairies' as Mum would put it. After about forty minutes more or so we kissed him goodbye and drove back to Roy Bridge.

Not a word was spoken between us for a good 30 minutes, until Mum asked if I could stop so she could have a smoke. I pulled over into the next parking layby and as we started to talk about the recent ordeal, we both started to cry like new born babies. I never was much of a crier but I was certainly making up for lost time today. This was a shock that nothing could ever prepare you for, nothing whatsoever.

After Mum finished her second cigarette we drove the rest of the trip in silence and I started to wonder what to do next. Silly question really, because what choices were there? We'd have to look for a care home in Fort William – and then there was the cost to consider. I had no idea how much they would charge, and up until now I had even thought of suggesting that Dad return home – after all, surely we could rally together and look after him?

Five minutes in the company of Dad made me I realise that idea was a non-starter. He had regressed so damn far that he obviously needed round-the-clock care, and we could not offer him anything close to that. Mum herself also needed a level of care that I doubted I could provide.

Not for the first time in recent days, I thought about Kalasin and the life that we were starting to build over there. Laid back, simple, and little of the stress that we'd experienced since returning to the UK.

I also felt no little resentment towards my darling siblings. Where the hell were they? Why was this down to me again?

Jum and Tom were waiting for us with cuddles and sympathy, and after telling them all about poor Dad all I wanted to do was have a sleep. The four-hour round trip, plus the whole New Craigs ordeal, had taken all of my reserves; I must have slept for a good five or six hours.

When I awoke it was dark, and after realising that it was after midnight I went to the kitchen to find Mum smoking her umpteenth cigarette of the day. We had a very long conversation and I explained to Mum that we needed to arrange a care home for Dad – and also that she would need to visit her own doctor, because it was clear that she needed some help.

Bangkok to Ben Nevis Backwards!

Ever since our arrival I had noticed that Mum would sit alone and make a low pitched moaning sound that would go on for hours. When I intervened, she would stop but she didn't take long before they returned. I think it must have been some kind of coping mechanism and after speaking to a few people who knew far more about carer's breakdown than I did, confirmed this for me.

You see, when it is just you and a dementia patient in the house, conversations are pretty hard to come by. To compensate for this, sometimes the carer will make some kind of noise to fill the gaps. God only knows how Mum had managed for quite so long.

Now Dad was never coming back, how hard it must be for her to get her own life together again! They had been together for some 50 years. Now all that had been snatched away from this lovely couple, to be replaced by a madness that could only be described as insane torture.

So it appeared that we had to somehow look to the future with a positive attitude and start to give something back to the people who had raised me.

Tom had started at Lochaber School and was already making friends quickly. He was doing okay at most of the subjects as well and was keen to stay late if any catching up was required. We visited Dad several times at New Craigs; Jum would come with us and Tom certainly wasn't afraid to come and visit his grandad.

Eventually we found a nice care home in Fort William called Moss Park, and after about four months, Dad was able to move in. The care home was about 30 minutes away from Roy Bridge, and we soon would visit Dad almost every day. Although it was clear that he was never going to be okay again, Dad seemed comfortable enough and soon got into a routine. It is incredibly important for sufferers of Vascular Dementia to follow a regular process, and this was exactly what Moss Park offered Dad.

I continued to write, and, with the tiny carer's allowance, we had enough money to get by, but it wasn't an ideal situation, and one day Mum took me to one side and had a word.

'Phil, you should go back to England where you and Jum can get proper jobs again.'

She explained that she could tell that we were not exactly thriving, and although she enjoyed our company, I could tell that she needed some space. When I passed these thoughts on to Jum and Tom they both seemed happy to consider the move, but they also voiced their concerns for Mum. These two caring people were putting others before them again, and I was so proud of them, so very proud.

It was clear that Mum would need some form of care, and after some stubborn arguing she came round to the idea. I called the same social worker who had helped us with Dad, and pretty soon a care package was put into place. Mum would receive four visits a day, beginning at about 8am, then at midday, the third one at tea time, and the final call would be around 9p.m..

'Och, I won't have any time for myself with these busy bodies knocking at the door every two minutes,' she complained, but I knew she was slightly worried about being alone once more.

By now it was December, and after speaking to Wallingford School about Tom taking up his studies once more, we made arrangements for somewhere to stay. The problem was that none of the local bed and breakfast places would put up with a small white dog. After calling in a few favours I found an old friend who would let us stay for a few weeks, which would be long enough for us to find a place to rent.

I had noticed that Mum would no longer come and visit Dad with us, and I asked her if she would be seeing him on a regular basis once we moved down South.

Mum looked at me as she drew back on cigarette number 20 for that particular day.

'Dear, I can't face seeing Colin in that state.'

I could see where she was coming from, but tried to explain that if it were *she* in the care home, Dad would visit every single day.

'I know that Philip, but I'm not as strong as your father was.'

I promised to at least come back up to see Mum every month, despite the 500-plus miles that would soon separate us. I couldn't bear the thought of Dad staying in Moss Park with not a single visitor.

'He doesn't even know who I am,' she continued, but I

knew that the more she visited him, the greater the chance of him at least forming some kind of bond with her.

MOSS PARK CARE HOME

We were due to leave in less than a week. After I was introduced to the care team I felt a little more comfortable with the whole shebang. Mum had very kindly paid for a 10-year-old car for us, and for that I will always be grateful. The day that we left there were plenty of tears, and although I knew that we had to go, a part of me still wishes that wasn't the case.

Once we had moved back to our lovely Wallingford, life began to get back to relative normality. I'd drive up to see Mum as often as possible, and every time I called into Moss Park there was a little less of Dad to experience.

Jum had convinced me to sort out some life insurance cover, Now that we were back in the UK Jum was mindful of the fact we had no property and hardly any savings to speak of. Life insurance has always been the archetypal 'Elephant in the Room' in our family, but now was the time to take it seriously.

'What would Tom do if we both die?'
'What happen if you die?'

What We've Become

'What will you do if I die?'

There was lots of talking about deaths, as you may have gathered.

My health had always been fairly good, despite the boozing and lack of exercise for the last 15 years... Okay, my weight was on the rise and I probably needed to start thinking about reading glasses, but nothing major. Jum was as strong as an ox, but there was a family history of illness that played on her mind.

So eventually I called one of the large companies, who sent a practitioner over to do some health check-ups on us both. I was mildly surprised when I opened the door to see a uniformed nurse smiling back at me, but in she came and pretty soon the testing began.

The health screening included testing for HIV, and although I was confident that we'd both be fine, that particular word always scared me. I suppose I remembered back to the days when HIV first became a household name, sometime in the mid 1980s. AIDs and HIV were synonymous with a death sentence, and I still recall the gaunt features of Freddy Mercury on the front pages of the daily tabloids. Eventually it became common knowledge that HIV didn't necessarily mean death, so long as it was diagnosed and treated in time.

So when the nurse produced a little stick and told me it was for testing for HIV, I gulped and opened wide.

The only other notable memory was when I produced my urine test and she commented that it was pretty high in sugar, according to her litmus paper.

The nurse was quite polite and told us, bar anything drastic, we'd get a letter in a week or so with the details of the policy. She was right in as much as a letter came for Jum, but nothing for me.

Two or three days passed before finally my letter was waiting for me as I opened the front door, after dropping Tom off at school. It was from the insurance company, but it wasn't a big fat one like Jum's. In fact, there were only a few lines of written content.

Essentially, they didn't want to insure me.

I started to feel a little faint. I sat on the floor and felt very alone.

So this was it. Somehow, I had managed to contract HIV.

Perhaps it was already full blown AIDS. Jesus Christ, what if Jum also had it?

Well, she didn't, according to the insurance health screening.

What pissed me off the most was the fact that they hadn't even got the good grace to tell me. There wasn't even an invitation to call the little sods.

After twenty minutes of self-pity, I mustered up the balls to call them.

Surprisingly, they answered fairly swiftly, and after being put on hold I found myself talking to one of the admin team, who had my medical notes in front of them.

'Mr Hall, we are unable to offer you life insurance based on the results of your health screening.'

This wasn't news to me.

'Please can you elaborate?' I asked, trying to sound as calm as possible.

'Unfortunately not. No, we would ask that you make an appointment to see your doctor.'

Oh God! So that was it then.

'Can you please answer me one question?'

All calmness had left the building.

'Of course, if I can.'

'Do I have HIV?'

There, I put it out on the line.

There was a pause.

'Mr Hall, the results of your HIV test…'

– *Oh go on then; just bloody well tell me now so I can make arrangements…*

'… are negative.'

Thank Christ!

I waited a few seconds and then breathed the biggest sigh of relief I'd ever experienced.

'So why do I need to go to the doctor?'

I guess he was on a roll, so he decided to let me know why they couldn't insure me.

And that was how I found out I was diabetic.

On a brighter note, Tom was doing very well in 6th form. He was more popular than ever, and was a constant source of joy for me and his mother. In fact, he was exceeding his objectives and we were told on parents' evening to expect some very decent grades. University beckoned for my son, despite the fact I'd selfishly removed him from the school that had now welcomed him back with open arms.

I eventually found work in a soulless call centre, and Jum got her old job back at the local hospital. Okay, we were renting, and were unlikely to ever get back on the property ladder, but that didn't seem so important any more.

Dad was becoming frailer every time I visited, and Mum seldom bothered to make the 10-mile journey. Occasionally I would bring my acoustic guitar and play a few songs; I just wanted to see that beautiful smile once more. I'd look into his dull eyes and see a poor soul imprisoned in a broken body. He wasn't having fun; he was barely alive – but seemed to be hanging on for something.

We were all in a kind of limbo, waiting for the inevitable.

Surely something had to give.

It was late spring in 2016 when I got a phone call from one of the nurses in Moss Park. I could tell from his tone that it was serious.

'Mr Hall, your father is very ill.' He went on to tell me that Dad had contracted a form of pneumonia, and they couldn't see him pulling through. His body was too weak to respond to the antibiotics.

I arranged for some time off work and drove up that evening. Mum sounded concerned, but shied away from visiting him. That really pissed me off at the time. Here was the black sheep of the family, despite being the least favourite, doing his best for his parents, and making everyone else feel bad about themselves – I hoped.

After the twelve hour drive I pulled up outside the care home, feeling a dull pain in my gut. It was similar to the time Mum and I had driven to New Craigs for the very first time. We'd had no idea what to expect, but we knew it would be an ordeal and a half.

I was shown to his room and gasped when I saw how tiny he had become.

The poor wretched man who had helped Mum bring me and my siblings into the world had never looked so vulnerable. What was left of his hair was sticking up. His mouth was open; most of his teeth had been removed, as they had become infected a few months earlier. There was a harsh

Bangkok to Ben Nevis Backwards!

rasp as he exhaled.

I asked the nurse to leave, and sat beside my father. I thought back to the times when I was ill as a child. Mumps, chickenpox, I had them all. Dad would make me chicken soup, and do his best to raise my spirits. Oh, how I longed for those days instead of this tragic role reversal that I found myself in!

Holding his cold bony hand, I stroked his cheek and prepared for the worst.

But it didn't arrive. About three hours later I was still there, and so was Dad. It was almost midnight. I decided I should go and say hello to Mum.

She was waiting in the kitchen, and we had a few drams together. It felt as if we were at a wake, but that the guest of honour was late.

Over the next three days I spent a lot of time by Dad's side. Every now and then a nun or priest would pop into the room and we'd talk about this and that. His condition hadn't worsened, but neither had it improved.

Eventually I decided that it was time to go back to my own family.

But Dad somehow pulled through, and defied all of the odds once more. The tough old bird was still alive, but I wondered – for what? Could he have any kind of enjoyment stuck in that frail husk? Reduced to being hand-fed and not even able to wipe his own backside? The Colin Hall that I once knew would rather be dead than taking part in that bloody freak show.

Don't get me wrong, the carers and medical staff do an amazing job – I couldn't do it – but what quality of life do those poor suffering souls actually get to experience once they lose the ability to look after themselves?

I wasn't close to Dad, but I still loved him as any son should love their father. We had some epic arguments when he was still sane, and some of the words that we exchanged would have lit up the dialogue of any action movie like a million fireworks in a dark room.

Mum used to put it down to us being so alike but that really wasn't the case. Dad liked his home comforts, and on the odd occasional when I had plucked up the courage to ask him out for a drink at the local pub, he'd just looked at me and said, 'Why?'

In retrospect, that was a bloody good question. What on earth would we talk about?

After Tom was born, I had hoped that surely, having provided Dad with a male grandchild who would carry on the Hall surname would have strengthened the our bond?

Wrong!

I can still remember when my son was about three years old and I saw him wander into the sacred living room where Dad was watching something like a rerun of *The Sweeney*, and tucking into one of his favourite mint imperials.

I heard Tom say, 'Grandad!'

Colin replied, 'What is it?' in an irritated voice.

'I'm hungry!'

Dad's considered reply was, 'Go and see your mother! Now leave me alone…'

This wasn't a sign of future dementia, far from it. Dad simply could not be bothered to indulge his grandson.

I was pretty peeved to say the least, but those words seemed a little too familiar.

Dad had worked away for as long as I could remember. Despite holding down a full time job, Mum was the one who brought us up. Even after coming back from South Africa, within a year or two, Dad had a job that meant we only saw him every other weekend.

By design? Of course. But despite this, he was my Dad and I adored him.

I suppose I just wanted to get his seal of approval, but that never came.

I asked Jum and Tom if they could come up in a few weeks' time. Jum was unable to take time off work, but Tom was happy to ride shotgun. He'd just about finished his 6th form and was looking forward to a long break. University was beckoning – he'd already been offered a few places on condition that his grades were good – but Tom quite fancied a Gap year. But for now, he had made some good friends during his time at school in Fort William.

In the end Tom and I never made the trip; something came up – I don't remember what it was.

But less than a week later, my father died in his sleep.

I took the call from one of the male nurses. He sounded genuinely sad; I remember he was a very decent fellow who went by the name of Craig, or was I confusing him with the name of the hospital up in Inverness? Anyway, I felt both sad and relieved when I hung up the phone.

Dad was free now. No longer was he trapped in that torture chamber of a body. Those frightened eyes were finally closed. His claw-like hands were hopefully relaxed and at peace.

Of course, I cried. More than I thought possible.

My lovely Jum immediately guessed what had happened, and was there for me, as she always had been. I was a lucky man. Even Tom came and gave me a manly hug.

I called Mum to break the news, but there was no answer.

I wondered how she would take it. Christ, it wasn't as if she'd seen him more than a handful of times since he had been in Moss Park. But despite that, I knew this would hit her hard.

I then called her number one carer, Annette, who answered almost immediately. She was going over to see Mum that morning and would text me when she arrived. Annette was a real rock, and I was grateful that someone would be there when Mum was told.

Although Dad's passing was awful, Jum reminded me that we were taking Megan for her bi-monthly haircut. Life does go on, as they say. The kennels where they offered this service was about three miles away, so we packed her into the car and made our way, in a somewhat subdued state.

I was just pulling out onto a fairly busy B road when my phone started to beep. Annette must be with Mum. I steered with one hand and stupidly attempted to read the text message. I could just about make out the first few words when Jum's screams rocked through my head:

'Philip!'

Looking up I could see that I'd veered across the white lines and was heading towards a pretty mean-looking truck. Thankfully I managed to swerve back over to my side of the road and no harm was done. This wasn't the sort of idiotic activity that I usually carried out. I waited for the barrage of shouting and reprimanding from my wife, but it never came.

We drove the rest of the way in silence.

Some time later I hung up the phone, saddened by how well Mum had taken the news of her husband's passing.

That was Dad's life, gone, and we'd never see him again... ever.

That afternoon I went to the local pub and ordered a large whisky. My friend who owned the pub looked a little concerned, and when I told him about Dad, he poured himself one and we sat down together. His own father had succumbed to dementia a few years earlier, and we shared some old memories, not all of them sad.

The next day I woke with a crashing hangover and a funeral to plan. The care home staff were very helpful – in fact, organising the entire day would have been a right pig without their help. I suppose they'd had plenty of experience.

The funeral was to be held on August 20th, 3 weeks after his passing. It seemed Mum would have a houseful. Father Tom would be taking the service, and he asked me about any eulogy arrangements. I decided I would bring my guitar and sing a song; seemed like a good idea at the time.

Dad hated my music. Even when he was literally out of his mind, whenever I played a song and mumbled a few lyrics I could sense his irritation. He would make a low murmuring sound that meant it was time for me to wrap up the whole thing. Simon Cowell would have loved to have Dad on the judging panel.

But I had decided some time before he died to learn a song that I knew he loved. Sadly, I never got the chance to sing it to him.

Because of the potential explosive nature of the bad blood between me and my siblings, I suggested to Jum that we stay in a local hotel.

I waited a week before trying to book a room for the three of us, but that was a mistake. It seemed that the whole world had decided to come to Dad's funeral. Of course that wasn't the case, but almost every room was booked for that weekend. Eventually I found a place in Fort William.

Organising a funeral is one of those tasks that not many people experience. For me it was a little weird because I had no idea how many people would be coming. Mum estimated between 10 and 100. I reckoned no more than 15 or 20 would be there.

She was calling up friends and relatives; the problem was

that most of Dad's friends would be seeing him real soon anyway – he'd outlived all of his army buddies. There'd be one hell of a party when he got there! (No offense intended to God.)

As for his relatives, well... Despite the fact that plenty of them had passed Fort William on their way between South Uist and Glasgow/Cambridge or wherever they lived, not one had bothered to visit him in Moss Park. Even the ones who had at least dropped in on Mum. Why the blazes should they be invited to his funeral? Well, that was my 'considered' opinion. But Mum did her best to invite as many as possible.

DAD'S FUNERAL

The next few weeks rushed by, and pretty soon we were en route to Glenspean Park to say hello to Mum and farewell to Dad. I had mixed feelings. There was relief that I would never again see that poor old man hanging on by a thread; there was sadness because I always felt this way at funerals.

The organisers of the funeral had told me that Dad's

body would be brought to the church that evening to be blessed. It was the standard procedure if the corpse had been kept in the mortuary for more than a week; Dad had been there for three.

I looked at my phone and noticed it was 17.30. Dad was due to rock up at 18.00.

As we walked up the path towards the Church doors I spotted Father Tom waving at me. He was a lovely old boy – 80 if he was a day, yet still full of life and always ready to crack a joke.

'Philip, have you brought your guitar?' I nodded and he beamed back at me. 'Your Dad would be so proud to see you today. The head of the family, you are.'

That was up for debate.

Father Tom explained that there had been a fatal traffic accident back in Fort William. We must have just missed it, because it was on the same road that we'd taken from the hotel.

'So, your father will not be joining us this evening.'

Blimey, that must be some jam!

I immediately felt guilty for discounting the poor dead cyclist. Apparently they hadn't found the motorist who had killed him (or her), and until they found sufficient clues, the road would be closed. This was both sad and badly timed.

After a brief chat with Father Tom, we walked back to the house. Mum excitedly told us that Martin had called; he was stuck in the traffic also. I hadn't seen my cousin since his father's funeral some ten years earlier. He'd made the drive up from Bristol, which was over 550 miles, which was very good of him.

Two other cousins, Gill and Suzanne, were also coming but they had met a similar obstacle when reaching Fort William. These cousins I hadn't seen for many years. Probably the last time was at Uncle Don's funeral in London back in the 1980s. Uncle Don was a really nice guy; his claim to fame was that he had been Prime Minister Edward Heath's personal bodyguard for some years.

After a mini-brainwave I asked Aunty Mary for Gill's number. If the road was to be closed all night their hotel was in Roy Bridge, they may as well have our rooms, since we couldn't get there from our side either.

The rest of the evening was pretty tame. Nobody was

Bangkok to Ben Nevis Backwards!

drinking, and we were all pretty bushed. Jum, Tom and I slept in the lounge, and at the crack of dawn Jum and I drove back to the hotel. The road had only been opened around 4 a.m. and I silently hoped that they would catch the person who had crushed that poor cyclist to death.

We bumped into my long-lost cousins on the stairway of the Ben Nevis Hotel. We exchanged pleasantries, and I realised that the last time we'd met, at least three of our Dads were still alive. Now they were all looking down on us, including Jum's father.

They were heading back into town, where their hire car had been left the previous evening. I dropped them off, and myself and Jum returned to the hotel for breakfast. The rooms had cost almost £100 each, so it had better be a bloody good effort!

To be fair, it did hit the spot. Replete, we packed up our stuff and I picked up my 12-string guitar to run through the song I was going to perform at the eulogy. I'd scribbled down the words and the chords on some paper, just in case.

By 9am we were back at the house and everyone had risen. Dad's body had been brought to the church and myself and Tom, went to the church to receive him. We were asked to attend a little blessing service that should have taken place the prior evening.

We were sat in the front row as they brought his coffin to the altar. Father Tom was dressed in his formal robes, and he started to talk a little about Dad. Almost immediately, my eyes filled with tears and I couldn't stop myself from crying. Tom asked if I was okay, but I just sat there blubbing away.

Thirty minutes later we were back at the house, and I was amazed to see that a massive spread of food had been prepared and laid out.

'Mum, who are you expecting?' I asked, and she just smiled, telling me that dozens were expected.

'Hi Philip!'

A familiar voice rang in my ears and I turned to see Martin. We hugged and chatted about losing our respective fathers, who were brothers. He explained that he and his wife Lesley had divorced, and he was now enjoying the life of a single man. Despite being at least 55, Martin seemed young and sprightly; clearly this status suited him pretty well.

They'd never had children. I thought about the kids that Dad and Uncle Ken had helped bring into the world, and their respective married statuses. The only ones that hadn't been divorced were myself and my cousin Rosalind, who was married in a civil partnership to Claire. The rest had all been through divorces, in some cases more than once. To be honest, these days it was a rarity to stay married more than 5 years.

'Let's go dear.' Jum was busying everyone to leave, and ten minutes later we were at the church to say goodbye to Dad for the last time.

I was pleasantly surprised to see that at least 25 people from the village had turned up. Some I knew and others I kind of recognised. Special mention should go to Andy, who would come and visit Mum at least once a month and would usually bring some cake.

It seemed surreal being at my own father's funeral. It was an event that I used to have nightmares about as a young child; I suppose that's not so uncommon.

This time, when Father Tom was talking about Dad, there were no tears from me. I thought that the truth was that he had long since died.

We sang a few hymns and before long, it was time for the eulogies. I smiled inwardly as I remember Father Tom asking me how long would my song be; he'd gone on to tell me about one eulogy which had carried on for a good ten minutes. I assured him that I would only sing two verses.

Showtime!

Perhaps not, but I was feeling pretty lively and was determined to give a heartfelt performance.

I warned the small audience that I was no singer, but I would give it my best. I then struck the opening chords to *Wonderful World* by Louis Armstrong, and took a deep breath. The song was warmly received, and I even managed to remember the words.

Twenty minutes later we followed Dad and his coffin out of the church and made small talk with the rest of the attendees. He was laid to rest in Cille Choirill cemetry, a beautiful Roman construction that had an awfully steep path leading to the graves. So steep, in fact, that Mum wasn't making the trip. This really saddened me, but she was probably right not to attempt it.

Bangkok to Ben Nevis Backwards!

Today was a beautiful day, and Dad was probably looking down on us and wondering where his Chrissie had got to.

Back at the house, it was clear that there was way too much food. About 20 people were present, and that included close family. I mingled, and was pleased to see both Jum and Tom were doing the same. Father Tom was the star of the show, and I marvelled at his wit as he seemed to be enjoying the moment chatting to much younger female guests.

The wake was a short one and in the morning we said goodbye to Mum and the few stragglers who were looking worse for wear.

I guess funerals are meant to be sad but this one made me feel a little happy. Dad was no longer stuck inside that human cage and was finally free. He was most probably playing scrabble with his beloved siblings, sipping on some decent malt whiskey and looking down smiling lovingly at the rest of his clan. Dad may not be in the ground, as Mum says now and then, but I am sure, wherever he is, he is still keeping an eye on us all and having a good old laugh to himself. See you soon Dad, but not too soon I hope!

We are still in Wallingford and Tom is doing well at Bournemouth University, probably enjoying the nightlife a little too much – but I guess he takes after his old man. He previously spent 3 months over in South East Asia enjoying his gap year travels before starting his degree course.

Jum is still the backbone of the family and dear Megan is also here to offer unconditional love when we need it the most.

Thanks so much for reading my story. You can email me at Dilbrain37@hotmail.com if you'd like to discuss the book, or anything else for that matter!

I have changed a few names and left people out for legal and ethical reasons.

the end

What We've Become

LAYING FLOWERS ON DAD'S GRAVE

TOM IN VIETNAM

About the Author

Phil Hall lives in Wallingford, Oxfordshire and currently works helping others to understand why IT is such a pain in the arse.

He shares his home with his lovely wife Jum and their adorable Westie, Megan and occasionally their amazing son, Thomas Hall.

This is his first published book and he plans to release a few more before admitting that perhaps he's better off raising tarantulas.

You can contact him on his website and he will be delighted to discuss the book or anything else for that matter except Arsenal Football club whom he detests!

WEBSITE: www.philhallbooks.com

Printed in Poland
by Amazon Fulfillment
Poland Sp. z o.o., Wrocław